ANIMAL CRACKERS

Book by
George S. Kaufman and Morrie Ryskind

Music and Lyrics by
Bert Kalmar and Harry Ruby

As presented by Arena Stage
May 1982

SAMUEL FRENCH, INC.

45 WEST 25TH STREET   NEW YORK 10010
7623 SUNSET BOULEVARD   HOLLYWOOD 90046
LONDON   *TORONTO*

HOORAY FOR CAPTAIN SPAULDING; words and music by Bert Kalmar and Harry Ruby, arrangement by William C. Schoenfeld. Author, according to the application for registration: Harms, Inc., employer for hire of William C. Schoenfeld. New matter: arrangement. Registered in the name of Harms, Inc., under E pub. 96275, following publication January 5, 1956.

THREE LITTLE WORDS; from "Check and Double Check," words by Bert Kalmar, music by Harry Ruby; with ukulele arrangement by S.M. Zoltai. Registered in the name of Harms, Inc., under E pub. 18483, following publication October 20, 1930. Renewed under R 203433, November 21, 1957, by Jessie Kalmar, as widow of the author, and Harry Ruby, as author.

WHO'S BEEN LIST'NING TO MY HEART; from "Animal Crackers," words and music by Bert Kalmar and Harry Ruby. Pianoforte and ukulele accompaniment. Registered in the name of Harms, Inc. under E 698961, following publication October 10, 1928. Renewed under R 157153, October 10, 1955, by Harry Ruby, as author. Renewed under R 157154, October 10, 1955, by Jessie Kalmar, as widow of the author.

EVERYONE SAYS I LOVE YOU; words by Bert Kalmar, music by Harry Ruby. Registered in the name of Famous Music Corp., under E unpub. 51507, following the deposit of one copy February 11, 1932. Renewed under R 230491, February 11, 1959, by Jessie Kalmar, as widow. Renewed under R 230492, February 11, 1959, by Harry Ruby, as author. Renewed under R 231123, February 11, 1959, by Famous Music Corp., as proprietor of copyright in a work made for hire.

EV'RYONE SAYS I LOVE YOU; words by Bert Kalmar; music by Harry Ruby. Song, pianoforte and ukulele accompaniment. Registered in the name of Famous Music Corp., under E pub. 30362, following publication May 21, 1932. Renewed under R 237068, May 21, 1959, by Famous Music Corp., as proprietor of copyright in a work made for hire. Renewed under R 246672, September 9, 1959, by Jessie Kalmar, as widow of the author.

KEEP YOUR UNDERSHIRT ON; from "Top Speed," words and music by Bert Kalmar and Harry Ruby. Pianoforte and ukulele accompaniment. Registered in the name of Harms, Inc., under E pub. 11152, following publication November 22, 1929. Renewed under R 181870, November 23, 1956, by Harry Ruby, as author and Jessie Kalmar, as widow of the author.

WHY AM I SO ROMANTIC; words by Bert Kalmar, music by Harry Ruby. Registered in the name of Famous Music Corp., under E unpub. 25824, following the deposit of one copy July 26, 1930. Renewed under R 196431, July 26, 1957, by Famous Music Corp., as proprietor of copyright in a work made for hire.

WHY AM I SO ROMANTIC; from "Animal Crackers," words by Bert Kalmar; music by Harry Ruby. Pianoforte and ukulele accompaniment. Registered in the name of Famous Music Corp., under E pub. 17822, following publication August 27, 1930. Renewed under R 198119, August 27, 1957, by Famous Music Corp., as proprietor of copyright in a work made for hire.

OH, BY JINGO; by A. Von Tilzer and Lew Brown. Included in "Animal Crackers" Copyright ©, 1946, 1974, by Broadway Music Corp.

LONG ISLAND LOW DOWN; from "Animal Crackers," words and music by Bert Kalmar and Harry Ruby. Registered in the name of Harms, Inc., under E 698959, following publication October 10, 1928. Renewed under R 157148, October 10, 1955, by Harry Ruby, as author. Renewed under R 157149, October 10, 1955, by Jessie Kalmar, as widow of the author.

SHOW ME A ROSE, OR LEAVE ME ALONE; by Bert Kalmar and Harry Ruby. For voice and piano. Registered in the name of Harry Ruby Music Co., under E pub. 76796, following publication December 21, 1953. Renewed under RE 91-851, January 5, 1981, by Charles U. Busch and Toby Garson, as children of Harry Ruby.

WATCHING THE CLOUDS ROLL BY; from "Animal Crackers," words and music by Bert Kalmar and Harry Ruby. Pianoforte and ukulele accompaniment. Registered in the name of Harms, Inc., under E 698960, following publication October 10, 1928. Renewed under R 157151, October 10, 1955, by Harry Ruby, as author. Renewed under R 157152, October 10, 1955, by Jessie Kalmar, as widow of the author.

FOUR OF THE THREE MUSKETEERS; Copyright © 1984, by the estates of Bert Kalmar and Harry Ruby.

ARENA STAGE
Washington, D.C.

Zelda Fichandler
Producing Director

Thomas C. Fichandler
Executive Director

ANIMAL CRACKERS

Book by George S. Kaufman and Morrie Ryskind
Music and Lyrics by Bert Kalmar and Harry Ruby

Directed by ....Douglas C. Wager
Choreographed by ....Baayork Lee
Musical Direction and Vocal Arrangements by ...Robert Fisher
Dance Arrangements and Orchestrations by ....Russell Warner
Dramaturg ....John Glore
Setting by...................................Zack Brown
Costumes by............................Marjorie Slaiman
Lighting by..............................William Mintzer
Technical Director ....David M. Glenn

THE SETTING

The Long Island estate of Mrs. Rittenhouse. The summer before
the Crash of '29.

ACT ONE

SCENE 1: Early Friday evening.
SCENE 2: Later that evening.
SCENE 3: Still later that evening.

INTERMISSION

ACT TWO

SCENE 1: Saturday afternoon.
SCENE 2: "The Professor's Dream."
SCENE 3: The party and pageant that evening.

Nancy Quinn
Associate Producer

Douglas C. Wager
Associate Director

May 8, 1982 — In the Arena

THE CAST

THE MUSICAL NUMBERS

ACT ONE

OPENING . . . . Hives & Butlers
HOORAY FOR CAPTAIN SPALDING . . . . Company
THREE LITTLE WORDS . . . . Wally & Arabella
WHO'S BEEN LISTENING TO MY HEART . . . . John & Mary
EVERYONE SAYS I LOVE YOU . . . . Ravelli & The Girls
KEEP YOUR UNDERSHIRT ON . . . . Captain Spalding &
                                        Mrs. Rittenhouse
WHY AM I SO ROMANTIC? . . . . John & Mary
†OH BY JINGO! OH BY GEE . . . . Jamison, Captain Spalding,
                                        Ravelli & The Professor
FINALETTO . . . . Company

ACT TWO

OPENING . . . . Hives & Guests
LONG ISLAND LOW DOWN . . . . Wally, Arabella & Ensemble
SHOW ME A ROSE . . . . Captain Spalding
WATCHING THE CLOUDS ROLL BY . . . . John, Mary &
                                        Ensemble
THE MUSKETEERS . . . . Jamison, Captain Spalding, Ravelli &
                                        The Professor
FINALE . . . . Company

---

†Music by Albert von Tilzer and lyrics by Lew Brown.

ACT ONE

SCENE: *Foyer of MRS. RITTENHOUSE's home on Long Island. OVERTURE.*
AT RISE: *Stage is empty. At opening HIVES comes down the stairs, pulls bell cord and BUTLERS enter.*
OPENING NUMBER: HIVES, BUTLERS, GUESTS. Music underscores the dialogue.

(*recitative*)
"Social season opens with
brilliant house party at the Long
Island home of Mrs. Rittenhouse."

"Captain Jeffrey T. Spalding,
noted explorer, returning
from Africa will be guest of honor."

"Roscoe W. Chandler, financier, will be in attendance."
HIVES.
YOU MUST DO YOUR BEST TONIGHT
BE ON YOUR TOES MEN
THERE'S AN HONORED GUEST TONIGHT
HE'S ONE OF THOSE MEN
WHO IS BEING FETED BY THE SMART SET.
BUTLERS.
WE'LL SEE THAT HE GETS WHAT HE DESERVES
HIVES.
AGAIN I MENTION
BE ON YOUR TOES MEN
HE CRAVES ATTENTION
HE'S ONE OF THOSE MEN.
MEN.
YES SIR, WE WILL GIVE HIM JUST WHAT HE
DESERVES.

(*MRS. RITTENHOUSE enters.*)

MRS. RITTENHOUSE. Oh, Hives.
HIVES. Yes, Madam.
MRS. RITTENHOUSE. I'd like to make a few changes in the assignment of the rooms.

9

HIVES. Very good, Madam.

MRS. RITTENHOUSE. Suppose you put Mr. Chandler in the Blue Suite?

HIVES. The Blue Suite?

MRS. RITTENHOUSE. That will leave the yellow for Mr. Winston.

HIVES. The Yellow for Mr. Winston.

MRS. RITTENHOUSE. Of course Captain Spalding as a guest of honor will have the Green Duplex, with two baths. I think the Captain would like two baths. Don't you?

HIVES. Yes, Madam. Having just returned from Africa he may need two baths. "Henri Doucet, art patron, will exhibit Beaugard's famous sculpture, "After the Hunt", at the party."

DOUCET. (*enters*) Ah, Madam.

MRS. RITTENHOUSE. Ah, Monsieur. So that's the famous Beaugard? I can't tell you how much I appreciate your kindness.

DOUCET. It is nothing. But it is all I have in the world. And so I lend it to you. For six weeks I have lived with it. I have slept with it. Tell me, what time do you expect Captain Spalding?

MRS. RITTENHOUSE. He'll be here very soon. Of course that's why I was so anxious to have the Beaugard here. (*to the BUTLERS*) Take it to the music room.

DOUCET. If madam does not mind, I would like first to lose myself in the mood of the room alone. (*exits*)

GUESTS.

WE ARE DYING FOR A DRINK

WE'RE GETTING NERVOUS.

BUTLERS.

WE WILL GLADLY POUR A DRINK

WE'RE AT YOUR SERVICE

GUESTS.

MIX IT WITH A KICK AND SERVE IT QUICKLY.

BUTLERS.

YOU WILL GET A KICK THAT YOU DESERVE.

ARABELLA. (*entering*) Well, mother, how is it going?

MRS. RITTENHOUSE. Very well, my dear. After this week, I don't think there'll be any doubt about who's who on Long Island. And it wouldn't surprise me if Mrs. Whitehead moved to Staten Island.

ARABELLA. Yes and that dippy sister of hers gives me a pain in the instep, too.

MRS. RITTENHOUSE. I do wish you'd take this more seriously.

Here you are a debutante. You've been out two months and you aren't engaged to a single person.

ARABELLA. What would you suggest, suicide?

MRS. RITTENHOUSE. I would suggest Mr. Winston.

ARABELLA. Huh?

MRS. RITTENHOUSE. Mr. Wally Winston. He's coming here today. Why not?

ARABELLA. Why not what?

MRS. RITTENHOUSE. Do stop fidgeting, Arabella. You know Mr. Winston's column in the Morning Traffic, the flaming forties, all about Broadway and Forty-second street, and Forty-third street? Everybody reads it, and everybody who is anybody is in it, and that's where you got to get.

ARABELLA. Oh, I'd love that.

MRS. RITTENHOUSE. Cultivate him a little. Furnish him with some gossip. You know the kind of thing he prints.

ARABELLA. Making whoopee.

MRS. RITTENHOUSE. Exactly.

(*HIVES enters.*)

HIVES. Mrs. Whitehead is here, and her sister Miss Carpenter.

(*MRS. WHITEHEAD and GRACE enter. HIVES exits.*)

MRS. WHITEHEAD. My dear Mrs. Rittenhouse.

MRS. RITTENHOUSE. My dear Mrs. Whitehead and Grace. So good of you both to come.

GRACE. Thank you.

ARABELLA. Yes, and it was pretty nice of us to ask you.

GRACE. Where are the distinguished guests?

MRS. WHITEHEAD. Yes, where is Captain Spalding? Hasn't he arrived?

MRS. RITTENHOUSE. Not yet, he'll be here presently.

MRS. WHITEHEAD. (*cattily*) You're quite sure he's coming?

ARABELLA. Oh yes, he doesn't know you're here.

MRS. RITTENHOUSE. He asked me to tell you, he's so sorry he can't get out your way. But of course with only one weekend at his disposal, naturally we can understand.

GRACE. A likely story.

(*HIVES enters.*)

HIVES. Monsieur Doucet is ready, Madam, to erect the sculpture.

MRS. RITTENHOUSE. Thank You. (*She starts toward exit. HIVES exits.*) I hope you'll pardon me. I am exhibiting a statue you know. Nothing important. Just Beaugard's little masterpiece, "After the Hunt". (*MRS. RITTENHOUSE exits.*)

ARABELLA. You'll have to pardon me too. Nothing important. George S. Bernard Shaw wants me to help him with his new play. (*exit*)

GRACE. Beaugard's "After the Hunt". Now where in the world did she get hold of that?

MRS. WHITEHEAD. Is it valuable?

GRACE. Is it? One of most famous in the world. When it was shown in Paris it caused a scandalous sensation.

MRS. WHITEHEAD. Sis, it looks as though we're licked for the season.

GRACE. It certainly does.

MRS. WHITEHEAD. Unless we can put this party on the fritz.

GRACE. There's an idea, let's bust it wide open.

MRS. WHITEHEAD. Now, let's see, what can we do?

GRACE. How about kidnapping Spalding?

MRS. WHITEHEAD. Who's Spalding? An elephant hunter. No wonder Mrs. Rittenhouse looks good to him.

GRACE. Cat. I've got it! The Beaugard. That's it!

MRS. WHITEHEAD. What?

GRACE. That sculpture she's got here.

MRS. WHITEHEAD. What are you going to do to it?

GRACE. Drive back to the house with me a minute. There's something we forgot to bring.

WINSTON. Well, Mrs. Whitehead I believe.

MRS. WHITEHEAD. You believe? Come home with me and I'll show you the license.

(*MRS. WHITEHEAD and GRACE exit. Enter TWO GIRLS.*)

FIRST GIRL. Why, if it isn't Wally Winston.

WINSTON. Hello, weakness. How are the heels today, any stronger?

FIRST GIRL. What's the news in town?

SECOND GIRL. Got any dirt for us?

WINSTON. What's the matter, didn't you read my column this morning?

First Girl. But that's old stuff now.

Second Girl. Yeah, we want the latest.

Winston. Tomorrow's column; sees all, knows all, and tells all.

(*WALLY and GIRLS exit. JOHN PARKER enters and puts down luggage and small crate, starts to come* DS., *hat in hand. HIVES enters looks at JOHN. JOHN looks at HIVES.*)

Hives. Someone you wish to see?

John. Yes, is Mrs. Rittenhouse in?

Hives. I'll see. (*takes up gold salver; extends it to JOHN*)

John. That's very nice. Yours?

Hives. May I have your name?

John. Parker, John Parker.

Hives. Of the Massachusetts Parkers?

John. No.

Hives. The Southern Parkers?

John. No. The Central Parkers. The bench at seventy-second street.

Hives. I see. I'll tell Mrs. Rittenhouse you're here. (*Exits. A pair of GUESTS cross.*)

John. Thank you.

(*MRS. RITTENHOUSE enters.*)

Mrs. Rittenhouse. Mr. Hoffman?

John. Parker.

Mrs. Rittenhouse. What is it I can do for you?

John. I guess it's my mistake. I thought you invited me here.

Mrs. Rittenhouse. I invited you?

John. I'm sorry, but I guess— (*He starts to get his things and leaves.*)

Mrs. Rittenhouse. Oh, of course. You're the young man who sculpts?

John. Yes.

Mrs. Rittenhouse. I met you at Mrs. Potters. We had that perfectly lovely talk about art.

John. Yes, I remember.

Mrs. Rittenhouse. So nice of you to come, Mr. Harper.

John. Parker.

MRS. RITTENHOUSE. Did you bring a sample of your wonderful work with you?

JOHN. Yes, actually I . . . this is . . . may I show . . . if you don't mind . . .

(*HIVES enters.*)

HIVES. Mr. Roscoe W. Chandler.

MRS. RITTENHOUSE. The very person I want you to meet.

(*FOOTMEN enter with luggage, golf clubs, etc. They stand at attention, while CHANDLER enters.*)

CHANDLER. Mrs. Rittenhouse.

MRS. RITTENHOUSE. Mr. Chandler.

CHANDLER. (*coming toward her with outstretched hands*) I'm so glad—

(*The splendid formality of this entrance is slightly marred at this point by the fact that CHANDLER trips over JOHN's bag which has been left c. He falls flat. The FOOTMEN halt with their luggage. HIVES come to help pick CHANDLER up. MRS. RITTENHOUSE and JOHN also are about to help. CHANDLER finally gets to his feet and butlers madly brush him off during the following.*)

CHANDLER. (*continued*) Who put that there?

JOHN. I'm awfully sorry I—

MRS. RITTENHOUSE. This is Mr. Parker, a young protege of mine. I've been so anxious for you to meet.

JOHN. (*his hand extended*) I'm pleased to meet you.

CHANDLER. (*brushing off his clothes at the time*) A pleasure.

MRS. RITTENHOUSE. Of course, I don't have to tell you about Mr. Chandler. Busy as he is in the financial world, he still finds time to lend a helping hand to the struggling young artist—

CHANDLER. I am just a lover of art, that is all. What people have given to me, I give back to them, in the form of beautiful things.

MRS. RITTENHOUSE. I do hope you'll be interested in Mr. Parker's work. He gave that exhibition last week—(*Her tone has been growing weaker.*) Didn't you?

JOHN. Why, no I—

MRS. RITTENHOUSE. Hives, show Mr. Parker to his room.

HIVES. Certainly, Madam. (*HIVES beckons to JOHN to follow him. HIVES and FOOTMEN exit with CHANDLER's luggage, leaving JOHN to pick up his own luggage and follow him off.*)

MRS. RITTENHOUSE. (*sitting at table L.*) Mr. Chandler, I think it's wonderful of you to give so much of your time to art. It must mean a great financial sacrifice.

CHANDLER. (*sitting at table L., opposite MRS. RITTEN-HOUSE*) Ah, but after all, money isn't everything. Suppose you work hard, and make eighty million dollars a year, by the time you pay your income taxes, what have you got left, seventy million.

MRS. RITTENHOUSE. That's life.

CHANDLER. You see, I am a lover of all kinds of art. The good kinds and the bad kinds. So long as it is art, I love it. I love it, because it is beautiful. I love everything that is beautiful, and that brings me to my point. You are beautiful.

MRS. RITTENHOUSE. (*rises to center*) Oh, no, Mr. Chandler.

CHANDLER. Well, maybe I'm wrong. (*takes her hand*) No, do not take away your hand. (*bends over and kisses it*) I love you.

(*ARABELLA enters.*)

ARABELLA. Oh, playing house?

CHANDLER. (*walking toward exit*) Well, two is company, but three is a corporation. (*exits*)

ARABELLA. Isn't that what Dr. Freud calls "Sex"?

WINSTON. (*enters, making a note*) Say, that's not bad. I think I'll use that in my column.

ARABELLA. In your Monday column?

WINSTON. No, Monday is special.

MRS. RITTENHOUSE. Tell me, what would Arabella have to do to get in the Monday column?

WINSTON. Well, she could make whoopee with some prominent person, like me.

MRS. RITTENHOUSE. (*walking L.*) If there's anything you're interested in, just ask Arabella. You would be surprised how much she knows.

ARABELLA. (*MRS. RITTENHOUSE exits. ARABELLA calls after her.*) And so would you.

WINSTON. What about this party? Anything in it for me?

ARABELLA. Don't you know? It's in honor of Captain Spalding, he's just back from Africa. (*sits on table*)

WINSTON. "Captain Spalding, the African Trail Tramper, is Long Islanding over the Week-end." Now, all I need is about five more items.

ARABELLA. That's terrific, Mr. Winston, the way you can just do that.

WINSTON. Thank you . . .

ARABELLA. Arabella.

WINSTON. Arabella, you can call me Wally. Got any hot tips? I prefer to work fast.

ARABELLA. You bet, Mr. Winston. "Did you know that Priscilla Alden was "that way" about Miles Standish? How's that for a hot item?

WINSTON. Not bad. I know a hot item when I see one.

ARABELLA. Thanks.

WINSTON. Your a born tipster, Arabella. Tell me more. I'm all ears.

ARABELLA. That's what I hear.

FIRST BOY. Captain Spalding is here. He just drove up.

FIRST GIRL. He's here, Captain Spalding. I just saw him. (*All on stage become quiet.*)

MRS. RITTENHOUSE. My Friends, Captain Spalding has arrived.

OMNES.
AT LAST WE ARE TO MEET HIM,
THE FAMOUS CAPTAIN SPALDING
FROM CLIMATES HOT AND SCALDING
THE CAPTAIN HAS ARRIVED
MOST HEARTILY WE'LL GREET HIM
WITH PLAIN AND FANCY CHEERING
UNTIL HE'S HARD OF HEARING
THE CAPTAIN HAS ARRIVED.
AT LAST THE CAPTAIN HAS ARRIVED.

(*Enter HIVES.*)

HIVES. Horatius Jamison, Field Secretary to Captain Spalding. (*This is spoken. HIVES exits. Enter JAMISON.*)

JAMISON.
I REPRESENT THE CAPTAIN WHO
INSISTS ON MY INFORMING YOU

OF THESE CONDITIONS UNDER WHICH HE COMES
  HERE
IN ONE THING HE IS VERY STRICT
HE WANTS THE WOMEN YOUNG AND PICKED
AND AS FOR MEN, HE DON'T WANT ANY BUMS HERE.
  OMNES.
AND AS FOR MEN HE DON'T WANT ANY BUMS HERE.
THERE MUST BE NO BUMS.
  JAMISON.
THE MEN MUST ALL BE VERY OLD
THE WOMEN HOT THE CHAMPAGNE COLD
IT'S UNDER THESE CONDITIONS THAT HE COMES
  HERE.
  HIVES. (*re-enters*) I'm announcing Captain Jeffrey Spalding.
  OMNES.
HE'S ANNOUNCING CAPTAIN JEFFREY SPALDING
OH DEAR HE IS COMING
AT LAST HE'S HERE.

(*SPALDING wearing a pith helmet is carried in a sedan chair
  by four NUBIANS. He gets out of the chair.*)

SPALDING. (*to one of the NUBIANS*) Well, how much do I
owe you? (*He gets an intelligible reply.*) What, from Africa to
here, $1.35. It's an outrage. I told you not to bring me through
Australia. That it was all torn up. You should have come right
up Eighth Avenue. Where do you come with that stuff? Turn
around the rear end. I want to see your license plates. I don't
think you fellows are on the square.

MRS. RITTENHOUSE. (*beginning a formal speech*) Captain
Spalding—

SPALDING. I'll attend to you later. (*calling after the departing
taxi-men*) Don't try to put that stuff over on me again.

MRS. RITTENHOUSE. Captain Spalding.

SPALDING. Who said that? Come outside and say that.

MRS. RITTENHOUSE. Captain Spalding.

SPALDING. (*finally greeting her*) Why, you're one of the most
beautiful women I've ever seen, and that's not saying much for
you.

MRS. RITTENHOUSE. Captain Spalding. Rittenhouse Manor is
entirely at your disposal.

SPALDING. Well, I'm certainly grateful for this magnificent

wash-out. I mean turn out. And now I feel that I ought to say
something.

SPALDING. (*sings*)
HELLO—I MUST BE GOING
I CANNOT STAY
I CAME TO SAY
I MUST BE GOING
I'M GLAD I CAME
BUT JUST THE SAME
I MUST BE GOING.

MRS. RITTENHOUSE.
FOR MY SAKE YOU MUST STAY
IF YOU SHOULD GO AWAY
YOU'D SPOIL THIS PARTY I AM THROWING.

SPALDING.
I'LL STAY A WEEK OR TWO
I'LL STAY THE SUMMER THROUGH
BUT I AM TELLING YOU
I MUST BE GOING

OMNES.
BEFORE YOU GO WILL YOU OBLIGE US
AND TELL US OF YOUR DEEDS SO GLOWING?

SPALDING.
I'LL DO ANYTHING YOU SAY
IN FACT I'LL EVEN STAY

OMNES.
GOOD!

SPALDING.
BUT I MUST BE GOING.

JAMISON.
THE CAPTAIN IS A VERY MORAL MAN.
SOMETIMES HE FINDS IT TRYING.

SPALDING.
THIS FACT I'LL EMPHASIZE WITH STRESS
I NEVER TAKE A DRINK UNLESS
SOMEBODY'S BUYING.

OMNES.
THE CAPTAIN IS A VERY MORAL MAN.

JAMISON.
IF HE HEARS ANYTHING OBSCENE
HE'LL NATCH-RALLY REPEL IT.

SPALDING.
I HATE A DIRTY JOKE I DO
UNLESS ITS TOLD BY SOMEONE WHO
KNOWS HOW TO TELL IT.
OMNES.
THE CAPTAIN IS A VERY MORAL MAN.
HOORAY FOR CAPTAIN SPALDING
THE AFRICAN EXPLORER
SPALDING.
DID SOMEONE CALL ME SHNORER?
OMNES.
HOORAY, HOORAY, HOORAY.
JAMISON.
HE WENT INTO THE JUNGLE
WHERE ALL THE MONKEYS THROW NUTS
SPALDING.
IF I STAY HERE I'LL GO NUTS
OMNES.
HOORAY, HOORAY, HOORAY.
(*pause*)
HE PUT ALL HIS RELIANCE
IN COURAGE AND DEFIANCE
AND RISKED HIS LIFE FOR SCIENCE.
SPALDING.
HEY, HEY.
OMNES.
HOORAY FOR CAPTAIN SPALDING
THE AFRICAN EXPLORER
HE BROUGHT HIS NAME UNDYING FAME
AND THAT IS WHY WE SAY, HOORAY, HOORAY,
    HOORAY.
SPALDING. (*spoken*) My friends, I am highly gratified at this
magnificent display of effusion, and I want you to know—
OMNES. (*sings*)
HOORAY FOR CAPTAIN SPALDING
THE AFRICAN EXPLORER
HE BROUGHT HIS NAME UNDYING FAME
AND THAT IS WHY WE SAY HOORAY, HOORAY,
    HOORAY.
SPALDING. (*spoken*) My friends, I am highly gratified at this
magnificent display of effusion, and I want you to know—

OMNES. (*sings*)
HOORAY FOR CAPTAIN SPALDING
THE AFRICAN EXPLORER
HE BROUGHT HIS NAME UNDYING FAME
AND THAT IS WHY WE SAY HOORAY, HOORAY,
HOORAY.

SPALDING. (*spoken*) My friends, I am highly gratified at this magnificent display of effusion, and I want you to know—
(*sings*)
HOORAY FOR CAPTAIN SPALDING, THE AFRICAN
EXPLORER
Well somebody's got to do it.

MRS. RITTENHOUSE. Captain Spalding, it is indeed a great honor to welcome you to my poor home.

SPALDING. Oh, its not so bad (*starts looking around*)

MRS. RITTENHOUSE. Needless to say, I—

SPALDING. Wait a minute I think you're right. It is pretty bad. As a matter of fact, it is one of the frowsiest looking joints I've ever seen. Where did you get your wall paper?

MRS. RITTENHOUSE. Why, I—

SPALDING. You're letting the place run down, and what's the result? You're not getting the class of people you used to. You're beginning to get people like you here now. Now I'll tell you what we'll do. We'll put up a sign outside, "Place under new management." We'll set up a seventy-five cent meal that'll knock their eyes out and after we knock their eyes out, we can charge them anything we want. (*takes paper and pen from pocket*) Now sign this here and give me your check for fifteen hundred dollars. And I want to tell you, Madam, that with this insurance policy you have provided for your little ones and for your old age, which will be here any day now, if I'm any judge of horse-flesh. And now, Madam, the time has come, the walrus said . . .

MRS. RITTENHOUSE. Captain Spalding, you stand before me as one of the bravest men of all times—

SPALDING. All right, I'll do that. (*stands in front of MRS. RITTENHOUSE*) Now what were you about to say?

MRS. RITTENHOUSE. Captain Spalding, you stand before me as one of the bravest men of all times.

SPALDING. Oh, that.

MRS. RITTENHOUSE. In the dark forests of Africa, there has been no danger you have not dared.

SPALDING. Do you mind if I don't smoke?

MRS. RITTENHOUSE. Fearfully you have blazed new trails, scornful of the lion's roar, and the cannibal's tom-tom. Never once in all those weary months, did your footsteps falter. (*SPALDING has by this time, assumed a heroic posture.*) Cowardess is unknown to you, fear is not in you. (*CHANDLER takes a caterpillar from SPALDING's coat.*)

CHANDLER. Pardon me, a caterpillar. (*SPALDING faints, falls. CHANDLER and MRS. RITTENHOUSE put SPALDING in a chair.*)

MRS. RITTENHOUSE. Oh, Captain! Put him here. Don't stand there, get the whiskey. Get the whiskey.

CHANDLER. Where is the whiskey? (*Noise from the crowd subsides.*) Where is the whiskey?

SPALDING. It's in my little black bag. In the right hand corner. (*The scene is broken by the sound of a trumpet outside.*)

MRS. RITTENHOUSE. What is that?

HIVES. (*enters and announces*) Senior, Emanuel Ravelli.

(*Orchestra plays, RAVELLI enters.*)

RAVELLI. Howda you do.

MRS. RITTENHOUSE. How do you do.

RAVELLI. Where is the dining room?

SPALDING. Say, I used to know a fellow, that looked just like you, by the name of Manuel Ravelli. Are you his brother?

RAVELLI. I am Emanuel Ravelli.

SPALDING. You're Emanuel Ravelli?

RAVELLI. I am Emanuel Ravelli.

SPALDING. Oh, no wonder you look like him. But still I insist there is a resemblance.

RAVELLI. Ha! Ha! He thinks I look alike.

SPALDING. Well, if you do, it's a rough break for both of you.

RAVELLI. (*to MRS. RITTENHOUSE*) Are you the lady of the house?

MRS. RITTENHOUSE. (*coming forward*) You are one of the musicians? But you weren't due until tomorrow.

RAVELLI. We couldn't make it tomorrow. It was too quick.

SPALDING. You're lucky they didn't come yesterday.

RAVELLI. We were busy yesterday, but we charge you just the same.

SPALDING. This is better than exploring. What do you fellows get an hour?

RAVELLI. For playing, we get ten dollars an hour.

SPALDING. Ten dollars an hour?

RAVELLI. Ten dollars an hour.

SPALDING. What do you get for not playing?

RAVELLI. Twelve dollars an hour.

SPALDING. Well cut me off a piece of that.

RAVELLI. Now for rehearsing we make you a special rate, fifteen dollars an hour.

SPALDING. That's for rehearsing?

RAVELLI. That's for rehearsing.

SPALDING. What do you get for not rehearsing?

RAVELLI. You couldn't afford it. You see, if we don't rehearse we don't play and that runs into money.

SPALDING. How much do you want to run into a open manhole?

RAVELLI. Just-a the cover charge.

SPALDING. Well, if you're ever in the neighborhood, drop in.

RAVELLI. Sewer.

SPALDING. Gee, we cleaned that up pretty good. Now let's see how we stand.

SPALDING. Flat-footed.

RAVELLI. Yesterday we didn't come — you remember, yesterday we didn't come.

SPALDING. Oh, I remember

RAVELLI. That's three hundred dollars.

SPALDING. Yesterday you didn't come, that's three hundred dollars. Well, that's fair, I can see that.

RAVELLI. Today we come —

SPALDING. That's a hundred you owe us.

RAVELLI. Hey, I think I'm gonna lose on the deal. Then tomorrow we leave — that's worth about —

SPALDING. A million dollars.

RAVELLI. That's all right for me. But I got a partner.

(*The trumpet is heard off stage again. The PROFESSOR is announced four times from off stage. Enter HIVES.*)

HIVES. The Professor.

SPALDING. It's probably the Professor. (*Music plays — the PROFESSOR enters.*) The gates swung open and a fig newton entered.

(*The PROFESSOR starts immediately up the stairs — there is a warning cry from those present. The FOOTMAN, carrying the baseball th:ngs, starts up the stairs, after him. The PROFESSOR ducks him; starts down again. The FOOT-MAN follows; the chase grows more rapid.*)

SPALDING. Don't let him do that to you, go for second. (*holding his hands to receive the ball*) Come on! Home! Home! (*The PROFESSOR slides into MRS. RITTENHOUSE, with the FOOTMAN close on his heels.*)
SPALDING. (*a wave of his arm*) Out!

(*The PROFESSOR throws his hat on the ground, comes to SPALDING, starts to argue. In pantomime he indicates that he was safe by three feet. RAVELLI also takes up the argument. SPALDING, to end the argument, starts to walk away. The two follow him, pulling him back, etc. SPALD-ING finally takes a stand; pulls out his watch.*)

SPALDING. (*continued*) I'll give you three minutes to clear the field. (*The crowd is yelling. Suddenly SPALDING misses his watch.*) Where's my watch? (*The scene now turns — RAVELLI and the PROFESSOR are scattering through the crowd, and SPALDING is chasing them. SPALDING finally catches the PROFESSOR.*) Give me my watch! (*The PROFESSOR exhibits a dozen watches. There's a rush from those present to reclaim their belongings.*)
MRS. RITTENHOUSE. Please! Please! . . . Hives, take the Professor's hat and coat.
SPALDING. And have him shown to the table.

(*HIVES removes the PROFESSOR's coat. His entire costume comes with it, leaving him only a loin cloth. He covers himself, immediately however, by taking the dress off the girl who is standing closest to him, thereby leaving her practically naked. There is a scream; the PROFESSOR reaches for another girl; the crowd scatters, he chases them off; everybody goes. Enter WINSTON and ARABELLA, giggling.*)

WINSTON. By the way, Arabella, how many children did you say Mrs. Fletcher had?

ARABELLA. She has four. Two by her first marriage and two before that.

WINSTON. Who would have guessed it? (*He writes.*)

ARABELLA. How am I doing so far, Wally?

WINSTON. Terrific. You're just terrific.

ARABELLA. I know.

WINSTON. Arabella, you know what I wish you'd do?

ARABELLA. Just say the word and consider it done.

WINSTON. See if you can get me some dope on Chandler. He's big game and you know I love to write about big guys: Lindbergh, Coolidge, Durante, Chandler . . .

ARABELLA. If there's anything to get, I'll get it for you. On one condition.

WINSTON. Just say the words darling and you've got it.

ARABELLA. *You* say the words, and you've got it.

WINSTON. I don't get it.

THREE LITTLE WORDS

ARABELLA.
I USED TO PAY NO ATTENTION
WHEN EVER I'D HEAR
SOME LONESOME ROMEO MENTION
"I LOVE YOU, MY DEAR".
NOW I WANT TO HEAR IT.
EACH TIME YOUR DRAW NEAR.
(*refrain*)
THREE LITTLE WORDS,
OH WHAT I GIVE FOR THAT WONDERFUL PHRASE.
TO HEAR THOSE THOSE THREE LITTLE WORDS
THAT'S ALL I'D LIVE FOR THE REST OF MY DAYS,
AND WHAT I FEEL IN MY HEART THEY TELL
    SINCERELY,
NO OTHER WORDS CAN TELL IT HALF SO CLEARLY.
THREE LITTLE WORDS, EIGHT LITTLE LETTERS
WHICH SIMPLY MEAN, I LOVE YOU.
    WALLY.
THREE WORDS IN MY DICTIONARY.
I NEVER COULD SEE,
BUT TO MY VOCABULARY
I'VE ADDED THOSE THREE.
I'M WAITING FOR SOMEONE TO SAY THEM TO ME.

(*refrain*)
THREE LITTLE WORDS,
OH WHAT I'D GIVE FOR THAT WONDERFUL PHRASE.
TO HEAR THOSE THREE LITTLE WORDS
THAT'S ALL I'D LIVE FOR THE REST OF MY DAYS,
AND WHAT I FEEL IN MY HEART THEY TELL
    SINCERELY,
NO OTHER WORDS CAN TELL IT HALF SO CLEARLY,
THREE LITTLE WORDS, EIGHT LITTLE LETTERS
WHICH SIMPLY MEAN I LOVE YOU.

(*After the number exit WINSTON and ARABELLA. Enter RAVELLI and CHANDLER, talking.*)

RAVELLI. Still I got the feeling someplace I have met you before. I don't care what your name is, I know your face.

CHANDLER. After all, I am one of the most well known men in America. The newspapers will keep running my photographs.

RAVELLI. I never see the funny pictures. Let me see, were you ever in Leavenworth, Joliet? Don't tell me, let me guess. Sing Sing.

CHANDLER. No, no you are entirely wrong. I spent most of my time in Europe.

RAVELLI. Europe? Ah, Czecho-Slovakia

CHANDLER. No, no you are mistaken, I tell you. I've never been there.

RAVELLI. Yes, Czecho-Slovakia.

(*GIRL enters, walks fast then runs and exits. PROFESSOR enters chasing her, but stops at top of stairs, as RAVELLI calls him, and crosses center.*)

RAVELLI. (*continued*) Hey, Byzon. Come here. You remember him, who was he? (*PROFESSOR shakes his head—NO.*) He comes from Czecho-Slovakia.

CHANDLER. You are wrong, I was never there. You are mistaken.

RAVELLI. I tell you, he came from Czecho-Slovakia.

CHANDLER. No, no, no, no. (*PROFESSOR looks him over. Then takes a fez and a beard from his pocket, applies them to CHANDLER.*)

RAVELLI. Papa? (*PROFESSOR imitates a fish.*) Ah, Abie the fish peddler.

CHANDLER. I tell you, it is not true. (*starts to reach for the beard, to remove it*)

RAVELLI. Leave it alone! Sure, Abie Kabibble, the fish peddler from Czecho-Slovakia. Wait! We'll prove it. Abie the fish peddler had a birth mark. (*birth mark business*) What did I tell you, Abie the fish peddler from Czecho-Slovakia.

CHANDLER. All right, boys, I confess. I was Abie the fish peddler. But don't tell anyone, please don't tell anyone.

RAVELLI. How did you get to be Roscoe W. Chandler?

CHANDLER. Say, how did you get to be an Italian?

RAVELLI. Never mind that. Who's confession is this anyhow? Put up your hands! (*CHANDLER does so.*) Higher! Higher! You can do better than that. (*The PROFESSOR takes out a gun and motions for CHANDLER to raise his hands still higher. Forces him to get on his tip toes.*) Well, of course we wouldn't tell anyone if it was worth our while.

CHANDLER. Of course, I am sure we can reach some agreement that will be mutually satisfactory. I can pay you well. You will be quiet, yes? Well now here. Suppose we say five hundred dollars? (*takes out money*)

RAVELLI. Five hundred dollars?

CHANDLER. Five hundred dollars.

RAVELLI. Piker. (*CHANDLER attempts to put the money back into his pocket, puts it in the PROFESSOR's pocket instead.*)

CHANDLER. That is all the cash I have with me.

RAVELLI. We take I.O.U.

CHANDLER. I am sorry but that is positively my best offer. That is all you will get.

RAVELLI. That's all we'll get?

CHANDLER. That's all you'll get.

RAVELLI. He's Abie the fish man! He's Abie the fish man! (*Business of PROFESSOR and RAVELLI running around.*)

CHANDLER. Please, please boys just a minute. Wait. I happen to have a check with me, which I received this morning, for five thousand dollars. Here I will give it to you. (*gives check to PROFESSOR*)

RAVELLI. Is it good?

CHANDLER. Of course it is good. Who would give me a bad check?

RAVELLI. I would.

(*The PROFESSOR looks at check and drops it on the floor, and the check bounces back in his hand. NOTE: RAVELLI works check with thread over CHANDLER's shoulder. PROFESSOR gives the check back to CHANDLER, shaking his head, "No". CHANDLER puts check in pocket.*)

CHANDLER. All right, if you won't take it, it is positively all I will give.

RAVELLI. Abie the fishman! Abie the fish man! (*PROFESSOR whistling. Business of RAVELLI and PROFESSOR running around.*)

CHANDLER. Please boys, please. What are you trying to do to me? (*Handkerchief business. CHANDLER discovers that his tie is missing.*) My tie, where is my tie? What happened to my tie? (*PROFESSOR hands CHANDLER a tie.*)

RAVELLI. Ha, ha, ha. That looks like—that is my tie. (*RAVELLI grabs tie from CHANDLER. PROFESSOR hands CHANDLER his own tie. CHANDLER discovers his teeth are missing.*)

CHANDLER. My teeth! Where are my teeth. Goniffs! (*PROFESSOR gives CHANDLER his teeth. CHANDLER storms off.*)

RAVELLI. Well you're a fine crook. All you got is a tie, a bad check and a bum set of teeth . . . (*PROFESSOR reveals the birthmark.*) And the birth mark. (*Both exit. Enter MRS. WHITEHEAD and GRACE, opposite.*)

MRS. WHITEHEAD. Believe me, if this little scheme works, it's the last party Mrs. Rittenhouse will ever give.

GRACE. Yes, and who gave you the idea?

MRS. WHITEHEAD. Yes, and who took it? Now be a nice little girl and run along and let your big sister handle all the dirty work.

GRACE. Aw, no, that's my department.

MRS. WHITEHEAD. Run along, my dear.

GRACE. Very well. I'll go and trample on some little children.

(*Exit GRACE. HIVES shows MARY STEWART into the room. JOHN enters opposite.*)

MARY. Hello, John.

JOHN. Mary, thank God. (*He catches himself.*)

HIVES. (*taking it in*) I see. The love interest.

MRS. WHITEHEAD. (*working her way toward the door*) And about time, too.

(*MRS. WHITEHEAD and HIVES exit. JOHN and MARY, as soon as they are alone, go immediately into each other's arms.*)

JOHN. Lord, but I am glad to see you. Where have you been?

MARY. Oh, the City Editor sent me on one of those assignments, but now everything is all right. Whatever happens here I can phone in.

JOHN. Anything? (*MARY nods. JOHN kisses MARY.*) Phone that in.

MARY. You know, "Among those present were—"

JOHN. Another ten minutes and I'd been among those absent.

MARY. I know these Rittenhouse parties—I've covered a dozen of them. By the way—where is she? I ought to say hello.

JOHN. Don't. She probably won't remember you.

MARY. She'll remember me all right. I'm the little girl that puts her picture in the paper.

JOHN. Gee, I wish I hadn't let you talk me into coming here.

MARY. Just the same, if you want to be a successful artist, these are the people you've got to meet.

JOHN. But it isn't worth it—I'd rather not have a career. What does Chandler know about art? And yet I'm no good unless he says so.

MARY. Listen dear, let's be fair about this. You don't think I'm enjoying it, do you?

JOHN. Mary, you know I love you. I'd do anything for you. But even if I go through with it, and Chandler gives me all the chance in the world, suppose then that I don't make good?

MARY. If you don't, all right. But we'll have had our chance.

JOHN. Last year I sold two sculptures. One brought me one hundred dollars and the other fifty dollars. Let's have a little common sense about it.

MEN. If you love me I don't care how much money you make.

JOHN. If I loved you.

WHO'S BEEN LISTENING TO MY HEART

IT IS NEEDLESS TO TELL YOU
THAT I LOVE BUT YOU
FOR I KNOW VERY WELL YOU ARE SURE THAT I DO.

MARY.
I HAVE KEPT OUR SECRET.
JOHN.
I HAVE KEPT IT TOO.
MARY.
YOU AND I CONCEALED IT.
JOHN.
BUT WHO REVEALED IT?
(*chorus*)
IT SEEMS TO ME THE WHOLE WORLD KNOWS I LOVE
   YOU
WHO'S BEEN LISTENING TO MY HEART?
SOMEHOW THEY SEEM TO KNOW I'M DREAMING OF
   YOU
WHO'S BEEN LISTENING TO MY HEART?
MY EYES HAVE SAID IT
THE FLOWERS READ IT
THE BREEZES SPREAD IT
THAT'S HOW IT STARTED
EVERYTHING SHOWS THE WHOLE WORLD KNOWS I
   LOVE YOU
WHO'S BEEN LISTENING TO MY HEART?
(*After number exit JOHN and MARY.*)

INTERLUDE

(*CHICO, at piano, with two attendants, plays and sings first
   verse of "EVERYONE SAYS I LOVE YOU".*)

RAVELLI.
EVERYONE SAYS, "I LOVE YOU"
THE GREAT BIG MOSQUITO
AND THE BEE STING TOO.
THE FLY WHEN HE GETS STUCK ON THE FLYPAPER,
   TOO.
SINGS "I LOVE YOU."

EVERYTIME THE COW SAYS, "MOO"
SHE'S MAKE THE BULL
A VERY HAPPY TOO.
AND THE ROOSTER WHEN HE HOLLER
COCK-A-DOOLY-DOOLY-DOO
SAYS, "I LOVE YOU."

CHRISTOPHER COLOMBO HE WRITE TO THE QUEEN
  OF SPAIN
A VERY NICE—A LITTLE NOTE

AND HES-A WRITE "I LOVE YOU, MY QUEEN"
AND THEN HE GET HISSELF A GREAT BIG BOAT.
HE'S A WISE GUY.

WHY YOU NO DO WHAT COLOMBO DO?
WHEN HES'A COME IN 1492?
HESAY TO POCAHONTAS, "ACK-E VACHI, VACHI
  VOO."
THAT MEANS, "YOU LITTLE SON-OF-A-GUN
I LOVE YOU".
(*All exit.*)

Scene Two

Scene: *Same. SPALDING and CHANDLER enter.*

Spalding. Yes, sir, Mr. Chandler, I've heard about you all my life, and I'm getting damn sick of it, too.

Chandler. And quite naturally, I have also heard of the great Captain Spalding.

Spalding. Well, that's fine, I've heard of you and you've heard of me. Now have you ever heard the one about the traveling salesman?

Chandler. (*laughing heartily*) Yes, yes.

Spalding. Well, now that I've got you in hysterics, let's get down to business. My name's Spalding, Captain Spalding to you.

Chandler. I am Roscoe W. Chandler.

Spalding. I am Jeffrey T. Spalding. I'll bet you can't guess what the T. stands for?

Chandler. Thomas?

Spalding. Edgar. You were close though. You were close though, and you still are I guess. Now, Mr. Chandler, this is what I wanted to talk to you about. How would you like to finance a scientific expedition?

Chandler. Well, that's a question.

Spalding. Yes, that's a question. You certainly know a question when you see it. I congratulate you, Mr. Chandler, and that brings us right back to where we were. How would you like to finance a Scientific Expedition?

CHANDLER. Is there any particular kind of an expedition that you have in mind?

SPALDING. Well, I'm getting along in years, now, and there's one thing I always wanted to do before I quit.

CHANDLER. What is that?

SPALDING. Retire. Now would you be interested in a proposition of that kind? My retirement would probably be the greatest contribution to science the world has ever known. This is your chance, Mr. Chandler. When I think of what you've done for this country. And when my baby smiles at me.

CHANDLER. Well, I've always tried to do what I could, especially in the world of art.

SPALDING. Well, I don't know how we got around to it, but what is your opinion of art?

CHANDLER. I am very glad you asked me.

SPALDING. I withdraw the question. (*to audience*) This fellow takes things seriously. It isn't safe to ask him a simple question. Tell me, Mr. Chandler, where are you planning on putting the new Opera House?

CHANDLER. Well, I thought I would put it somewhere near Central Park.

SPALDING. Why not put it right in Central Park?

CHANDLER. Could we do that?

SPALDING. Sure, if you kept off the grass. Why not put it in the reservoir, and get the whole thing over with. Of course that would interfere with the water supply, but we must remember that art is art. Still, on the other hand, water is water, and East is East and West is West and Coolidge is president. And if you take Cranberries and stew them like rhubarb, they make much better apple sauce than prunes do. Now you tell me what you know.

CHANDLER. I would like very much to give you my opinions.

SPALDING. I'll ask you for them sometime. Remind me, will you? Tell me, Mr. Chandler, what do you think of the Stock Market?

CHANDLER. Well, in the first place it is a Presidential year.

SPALDING. Isn't it though. Remember the year we had the locusts? I voted for them too. What do you think of the traffic problem? What do you think of the marriage problem? What do you think of at night when you go to bed, you beast?

CHANDLER. Well, I'll tell you —

SPALDING. I'd rather not hear any more about it. Remember, there are traveling salesmen present.

CHANDLER. Well, Captain in the last analysis, it is a question of money. You see the nickel today is not what it used to be ten years ago.

SPALDING. I'll go further than that. I'll get off at Times square. It's not what it was fifteen years ago. Do you know what this country needs today?

CHANDLER. What?

SPALDING. A seven cent nickel. It would solve the whole subway problem. We've been using the five-cent nickel in this country since fourteen ninety two. That's roughly two hundred years, daylight saving. Why not give the seven-cent nickel a chance. If that works out, next year we can have an eight-cent nickel. You could go to a news-stand buy a three-cent paper, and get the same nickel back. One nickel carefully used, could last a family a lifetime.

CHANDLER. Captain Spalding, I think that is a wonderful idea.

SPALDING. You do, eh?

CHANDLER. Yes.

SPALDING. Well, than there can't be too much to it. Forget about it.

CHANDLER. Tell me — Captain Chandler — er, Spalding —

SPALDING. Yes, Spalding. You're Chandler. You're Chandler and I'm Spalding. It's the switching from the light to the heavy underwear. You're Chandler and I'm Spalding. Let's have no more of that either. Weren't you on the daisy chain at Vassar years ago? I've seen you on some chain, I don't know where it was.

CHANDLER. Tell me, Captain — er — er —

SPALDING. Spalding. You're Chandler and I'm Spalding. (*to audience*) Could I see a program a minute? It might be intermission for all he knows.

CHANDLER. Tell me Captain Spalding, you've been quite a traveler, what do you think we ought to do about South America? It is a big problem, South America. I really don't know what to do about it.

SPALDING. Say, you're in a nasty fix.

CHANDLER. As a matter of fact, I'm going down there very soon.

SPALDING. Is that so? Where are you going?

CHANDLER. Uruguay.

SPALDING. Uruguay? Well, you go Uruguay and I'll go mine.

CHANDLER. But what about Guatemala?

SPALDING. Well, that's totally different problem. Guatemala every night or you can't Mala at all. Of course, that takes a lot of Honduras. How did this ever start anyhow? Let's talk about something else. Take the Foreign situation. Take Abyssinia. I'll tell you what. You take Abyssinia and I'll take a butterscotch sundae on rye bread. No make mine the same. Pardon me, my name is Spalding. I've always wanted to meet you. Let's see what the boys in the back room will have. (*SPALDING and CHAND-LER exit.*)

EVERYONE SAYS I LOVE YOU

RAVELLI and the FOUR HAREM GIRLS.
EVERYONE SAYS "I LOVE YOU",
THE COP ON THE CORNER,
AND THE BURGLAR, TOO.
THE PREACHER IN THE PULPIT,
AND THE MAN IN THE PEW
SAYS "I LOVE YOU."
EVERYONE, NO MATTER WHO,
THE FOLKS OVER EIGHTY
AND THE KID OF TWO;
THE CAPTAIN AND THE SAILOR
AND THE REST OF THE CREW
SAYS, "I LOVE YOU".
THERE ARE ONLY EIGHT LITTLE LETTERS
IN THIS PHRASE, YOU'LL FIND
BUT THEY MEAN A LOT MORE THAN
ALL THE OTHER WORDS COMBINED.
EVERYWHERE, THE WHOLE WORLD THROUGH,
THE KING IN THE PALACE
AND THE PEASANT, TOO.
THE TIGER IN THE JUNGLE
AND THE MONK IN THE ZOO,
SAYS, "I LOVE YOU."

(*The PROFESSOR enters and chases the HAREM GIRLS off.*)

SCENE THREE

SCENE: *The Drawing Room. The same evening. Beaugard's "After the Hunt", veiled above the doorway, over french doors.*

RAVELLI. Come here. That's all you do. Chase the women. Look! Everybody else play cards. They no ask us. Here we are, waste all time. We been here all day. How much we make. Not enough to pay over-the-head. We no careful, we got to live on charity. Then we have to go to Old Ladies home. How you like that? (*PROFESSOR indicates "yes".*) No, no, that's no good. (*fight business*) Can't take it, huh? Everybody here got plenty of money. We to make some money. We got to get somebody to play with us. I play anything. Poker, Polo, tag— (*THE PRO-FESSOR tags him and starts to run away. At that moment MRS. RITTENHOUSE enters; the PROFESSOR tags her.*)

MRS. RITTENHOUSE. (*innocently laying a hand on RAVELLI's arm*) Oh, Signor Ravelli—

RAVELLI. That makes me it. (*runs after the PROFESSOR*) Now you it.

(*Enter MRS. WHITEHEAD. The PROFESSOR immediately runs over and tags her—with a resounding slap.*)

MRS. WHITEHEAD. I beg your pardon! (*knee business*) What's the matter with his feet? (*PROFESSOR pulls out a chemise from MRS. WHITEHEAD's bosom with his teeth. MRS. WHITEHEAD screams as PROFESSOR shows the chemise to audience and then puts it in his pocket.*)

RAVELLI. We play all kindsa games. Black-jack. (*PRO-FESSOR takes black-jack from pocket.*) Soccer. (*PROFESSOR attempts to hit MRS. WHITEHEAD.*)

MRS. RITTENHOUSE. Here, here, what are you doing?

(*MRS. RITTENHOUSE and MRS. WHITEHEAD start to-ward the couch. MRS. RITTENHOUSE is about to sit down. PROFESSOR is under her and she sits in PROFES-SOR's lap. She screams and rises. PROFESSOR moves to left of couch. MRS. WHITEHEAD sits on couch right. PROFESSOR throws his right leg over on MRS. WHITE-HEAD's lap. She throws it back. He repeats it. He then*

throws both legs over on MRS. WHITEHEAD's lap. She
throws them back. He repeats it. He then throws one leg
over shoulder and one leg on lap. Then PROFESSOR and
RAVELLI intertwine legs and arms. PROFESSOR then
raises MRS. WHITEHEAD's legs. She screams and rises.
PROFESSOR does fight business with MRS. RITTEN-
HOUSE.)

Mrs. Rittenhouse. (*continued*) Hives, where are you? Oh,
Hives, where are you? (*Gong rings off stage as PROFESSOR*
falls in chair. RAVELLI fans him. MRS. RITTENHOUSE and
MRS. WHITEHEAD ad lib. Gong rings again. PROFESSOR
again goes into fight scene with MRS. RITTENHOUSE.) Here
he comes again. Oh, Hives, Hives. (*PROFESSOR tries to em-*
brace MRS. RITTENHOUSE. She pushes him away.)

Ravelli. Well, why don't you leave him alone. (*PROFESSOR*
does leg business with RAVELLI.) Now that the game is over,
how about playing some bridge? You play bridge?

Mrs. Rittenhouse. Well, I play bridge a little.

Ravelli. How much you play for?

Mrs. Rittenhouse. Oh, we just play for small stakes.

Ravelli. And french fried potatoes? (*Enter HIVES with*
folding card table.)

Mrs. Rittenhouse. Set it up right over there, Hives.

(*HIVES begins opening table. As he opens each leg of the table*
the PROFESSOR standing at his right pushes the leg closed
again with his foot. This business is repeated until center
of table falls out.)

Hives. Extraordinary!

Mrs. Rittenhouse. It's all right, Hives, we'll just sit here.

(*HIVES exits with table. MRS. RITTENHOUSE, MRS.*
WHITEHEAD and RAVELLI sit at table, PROFESSOR
pulls table away from them, to center. All follow PRO-
FESSOR with chairs and put them at table. Positions for
card game: PROFESSOR left, RAVELLI right, MRS.
RITTENHOUSE back of table, facing audience, MRS.
WHITEHEAD opposite MRS. RITTENHOUSE, with back
to audience.)

RAVELLI. Now, how do you want to play, honest?

MRS. RITTENHOUSE. I hope so. Come along now, we'll all cut for partners.

RAVELLI. He's my partner, that's the only way we play.

MRS. RITTENHOUSE. I'm sorry it's against the rules. We'll have to cut for partners.

RAVELLI. All right, we'll cut for partners. (*MRS. RITTEN-HOUSE spreads the cards, they all pick one.*) I got ace of spades. (*The PROFESSOR shows them his card.*) He's got ace of spades.

MRS. RITTENHOUSE. Two aces of spades?

RAVELLI. Two? He's got thousands of them.

MRS. RITTENHOUSE. Well, I suppose that gives him the choice of seats.

MRS. WHITEHEAD. You have the choice of seats. (*The PRO-FESSOR sits in MRS. RITTENHOUSE's lap.*)

MRS. RITTENHOUSE. Not on her lap!

RAVELLI. He thought it was contact bridge. (*PROFESSOR looks at a few cards on top of the deck, puts them back and starts to deal.*)

MRS. WHITEHEAD. Shuffle the cards.

RAVELLI. You know, just scrumble 'em up a bit. (*The PRO-FESSOR does a fake shuffle. He passes the deck to RAVELLI to cut. RAVELLI indicates that he doesn't want to cut. PRO-FESSOR takes the cards and starts to deal again. MRS. RIT-TENHOUSE stops him, and asks to cut the cards.*)

MRS. RITTENHOUSE. I want to cut the cards. (*THE PRO-FESSOR gives her the cards, she cuts, he puts the two halves back as they originally were, then he starts to deal. Wetting the right thumb, but dealing with the left hand. During the deal he drops the card. MRS. WHITEHEAD picks it up and lays it on the table. THE PROFESSOR slaps her hand for doing so.*)

RAVELLI. All right, you bid, partner. No spades, no spades partner. (*PROFESSOR passes.*) You pass? Mis-deal.

MRS. RITTENHOUSE. I don't understand this kind of bidding. (*MRS. RITTENHOUSE lays her cards on the table, and the PROFESSOR immediately switches his cards with her. MRS. RITTENHOUSE picks up PROFESSOR's cards, thinking they are her own.*) Why, these are not my cards.

MRS. WHITEHEAD. There's something wrong here. I want to go over the bidding.

MRS. RITTENHOUSE. You put that right away. Well, it's your own fault.

RAVELLI. (*to PROFESSOR*) Hey, she wants you to start 'em up again. (*PROFESSOR indicates one.*) He bids one.

MRS. WHITEHEAD. One? One what?

RAVELLI. That's all right, you find out.

MRS. RITTENHOUSE. But we have to know what he's bidding.

RAVELLI. We tell you later. I bid two.

MRS. RITTENHOUSE. Two what?

RAVELLI. Two the same as he's bidding. That's enough bidding, dummy leads. Dummy leads.

MRS. RITTENHOUSE. I'm not the dummy.

RAVELLI. Okay you lead.

MRS. WHITEHEAD. What shall I lead?

RAVELLI. Lead anything. (*WHITEHEAD leads.*) You can't lead that.

MRS. WHITEHEAD. Why not?

RAVELLI. Because we can't take it.

MRS. RITTENHOUSE. I insist on knowing what is trump.

RAVELLI. What do you care? You can't start an argument in the middle of the game.

(*An argument among all four ensues, and the card game breaks up. THE PROFESSOR heads toward exit, revealing that he now wears MRS. WHITEHEAD's high-heels. MRS. WHITEHEAD chases him off, clumping after him in THE PROFESSOR's worn-out shoes. RAVELLI follows. CAPTAIN SPALDING enters as they exit, and takes note of their shoes. He takes a puzzled look at his own shoes, then turns to MRS. RITTENHOUSE.*)

SPALDING. Mrs. Rittenhouse, yoo hoo, are we alone?

MRS. RITTENHOUSE. Why Captain—I don't understand—

SPALDING. Don't understand being alone? Don't give me that innocent stuff—or you'll be alone. (*MRS. RITTENHOUSE shrinks away from him.*) A big cluck like you turning cute on me. Come out here in the arena. I'm a man that likes to roam around, Mrs. Ritten—

MRS. RITTENHOUSE. Mrs. Ritten?

SPALDING. I haven't got time for the whole thing. I'm a busy man. Mrs. Rittenhouse, ever since I met you I've swept you off my feet. Something has been throbbing within me. Oh, it's been beating like the incessant tom-tom in the primitive jungle. There's something that I must ask you.

MRS. RITTENHOUSE. What is it, Captain?

SPALDING. Would you wash out a pair of socks for me?

MRS. RITTENHOUSE. Why Captain, I'm surprised.

SPALDING. It may be a surprise to you, but it's been on my mind for months. It's just my way of telling you that I love you, Mrs. Rittenhouse, I love you, I love you, I love you.

KEEP YOUR UNDERSHIRT ON

SPALDING.
TELL ME, WHY IS IT, WHEN YOU'RE NEAR
PASSION JUST OVERCOMES ME.
SOMETHING ABOUT YOU NUMBS ME?
TELL ME, WHY DO I FEEL SO QUEER?
EVERYTIME YOU APPEAR I GET LIKE THIS
WANNA HUG AND KISS.

CURB YOUR EMOTION,
DON'T GO OFF YOUR NUT,
I'VE GOT A NOTION I COULD LOVE YOU,
BUT DON'T GET EXCITED,
KEEP YOUR UNDERSHIRT ON.

MRS. RITTENHOUSE.
I'VE NO OBJECTION TO A HUG OR TWO,
I LIKE AFFECTION
BUT I'M WARNING YOU.

SPALDING.
DON'T GET EXCITED
KEEP YOUR UNDERSHIRT ON.
I ALWAYS LET THE GIRLS KISS ME
IF THEY LIKE IT
AND THEY LIKE IT.
I'M WISE TO ALL THE TRICKS THEY SPRING
MY MOTHER TOLD ME EVERYTHING.
THOUGH YOU'LL UPSET ME
THAT'S A CHANCE I'LL TAKE
GO ON AND PET ME
BUT FOR HEAVENS SAKE
DON'T GET EXCITED
KEEP YOUR UNDERSHIRT ON.

(*After number, exit SPALDING and MRS. RITTENHOUSE. Enter GRACE and CHANDLER.*)

GRACE. You've never met anyone like me, have you?

CHANDLER. The very words I was about to say.

GRACE. You know we were fated to meet. The minute I read about your income—

CHANDLER. Oh, you know about my income?

GRACE. I know all about your various interests. Finance, painting, music and art.

CHANDLER. Ah, but you have left one out. One that will surprise you. I am the anonymous owner of the Morning Traffic.

GRACE. So, a maverick newspaper owner, too. Don't you ever find time for anything except work?

CHANDLER. Well, sometimes I—

GRACE. You do. You dear old-fashioned thing.

(*Enter WINSTON.*)

WINSTON. Ah, something for the column. (*writes*) "Financial wizard in sex orgy". Do you mind?

GRACE. Mind? I love it.

CHANDLER. Very well said, my dear.

(*Exit CHANDLER and GRACE. Enter ARABELLA.*)

ARABELLA. Oh Wally, Wally! I just learned something wonderful.

WINSTON. (*not quite interested*) Really, what?

ARABELLA. I overheard that Italian talking to his partner. It's about Chandler.

WINSTON. (*interested*) Yeah?

ARABELLA. His name isn't Chandler at all. It's Abie Kabbible, the fish peddler from Czecho-Slovakia.

WINSTON. He—what? (*He glances in the direction of CHANDLER's exit. Turns ARABELLA, and impulsively folds her in his arms and kisses her until she is breathless.*)

ARABELLA. Wally, what are you doing?

WINSTON. Don't you know?

ARABELLA. No. (*He kisses her again.*)

WINSTON. There! Will you marry me.

ARABELLA. If you insist.

WINSTON. Imagine, Roscoe W. Chandler a fish peddler. That's the kind of stuff they're crazy about at the paper. Do you know what they'll do, they'll probably give me a huge bonus.

ARABELLA. Oh, Wally, and I did it all.

WINSTON. You bet you did. Where is that phone. I can still get the Chandler item in tomorrow's Traffic if I hurry up. Say, wait till that big ham reads this.

(*ARABELLA and WALLY exit. JOHN and MARY enter.*)

MARY. Well, so this is the famous Beaugard. You've seen it, haven't you?

JOHN. Seen it? I sat in front of it three weeks copying it.

MARY. You did.

JOHN. Me, and a couple dozen other promising young sculptors.

MARY. Well, I'll bet your copy was better than any of them.

JOHN. It wasn't bad at that. Actually, I brought it with me to try to sell to Mrs. Rittenhouse. But now . . .

MARY. John. You're so . . . I've got an idea.

JOHN. What?

MARY. Listen, they're going to unveil the Beaugard tonight, aren't they?

JOHN. Yes.

MARY. Suppose—suppose when they unveil it, they don't find the Beaugard there, but find yours?

JOHN. You mean put mine—

MARY. Exactly.

JOHN. Mary, we couldn't do that.

MARY. Yes, we could. It's our big chance. Don't you see? The sculpture is unveiled, they all admire it and then after they've hailed the artist, we'll tell them who he really is.

JOHN. But suppose they don't hail the artist? Suppose they hate it?

MARY. Isn't the chance worth taking? Think what it means.

JOHN. We can't do it.

MARY. What are you afraid of? Marrying me? (*Music begins and continues under the following dialogue leading into song.*)

JOHN. Gee, that'd be wonderful.

MARY. That's what it means if it works.

JOHN. That'd change everything. Mary, that'd be wonderful.

MARY. John dear, you're going to have a wonderful future.

WHY AM I SO ROMANTIC?

MARY.
ALL THE BOYS I'VE KNOWN USED TO SAY
I WAS MADE OF STONE.
I WOULD ALWAYS LEAVE THEM ALONE IN DESPAIR
I WAS ON THE PAN
I'VE BEEN CALLED AN ELECTRIC FAN,
TOLD I'M EVEN COLDER THAN FRIGIDAIRE.
I BEGAN TO WONDER IF I WAS ALL WRONG.
I THOUGHT SO TIL YOU CAME ALONG.
(*refrain*)
TELL ME DEAR, WHY AM I SO ROMANTIC?
WHEN YOU'RE NEAR, WHY AM I SO ROMANTIC?
WHAT A GRAND FEELING WHEN YOUR LIPS MEET
   MINE,
THAT CERTAIN SOMETHING COMES STEALING UP
   AND DOWN MY SPINE.

I DON'T KNOW WHAT IT IS YOU DO TO ME
YOU DON'T KNOW HALF O' THE GOOD YOU DO ME
OTHER BOYS BORE ME
THEY JUST LEAVE ME BLUE BUT
WHY AM I SO ROMANTIC WITH YOU?
   JOHN.
TELL ME DEAR, WHY AM I SO ROMANTIC?
WHEN YOU'RE NEAR, WHY AM I SO ROMANTIC?
WHAT A GRAND FEELING WHEN YOUR LIPS MEET
   MINE.
THAT CERTAIN SOMETHING COMES STEALING UP
AND DOWN MY SPINE.
   MARY.
WHEN WE PET CLOSER YOUR ARMS DO HOLD ME
I FORGET ALL THAT MY MOTHER TOLD ME.
   JOHN.
OTHER GIRLS BORE ME
THEY JUST LEAVE ME BLUE.
   BOTH.
BUT WHY AM I SO ROMANTIC WITH YOU?

(*Exit after number, girl enters, and exits followed by PRO-*

FESSOR. RAVELLI enters and is looking around for PROFESSOR and MARY enters.)

MARY. Oh, Mr. Raviolli,

RAVELLI. Ravelli

MARY. There is something I want you to do for me.

RAVELLI. I'd do anything you want.

MARY. Do you mean that?

RAVELLI. What do you think? I talk just to hear myself say nothing?

MARY. (*indicating statue*) Do you see that statue?

RAVELLI. (*indicating statue*) You mean this statue?

MARY. Yes. I want you to take that one down, and put another one in its place.

RAVELLI. I don't know what you mean, but I'll do it.

MARY. I mean I want you to take that statue away, and put this one in its place.

RAVELLI. You mean, you want me to steal this statue up there and put this one in its place? You want I should steal.

MARY. Oh no, it's not stealing.

RAVELLI. Well, than I couldn't do it.

(*As they both exit, HIVES enters through French doors with an accompanying flash of lightning and thunder. MRS. WHITEHEAD enters.*)

MRS. WHITEHEAD. Oh, hello Hives. It certainly seems strange to see you any place but in our own home.

HIVES. I miss you too, Mrs. Whitehead. (*thunder*)

MRS. WHITEHEAD. Well, it looks as though we're in for a storm, doesn't it?

HIVES. I'm afraid so, Mrs. Whitehead. (*thunder*)

MRS. WHITEHEAD. So that's the famous sculpture, is it?

HIVES. Yes, Mrs. Whitehead.

MRS. WHITEHEAD. Hives, do you still feel there is a strong bond between us?

HIVES. Indeed yes.

MRS. WHITEHEAD. Strong enough for you to do me a big favor?

HIVES. Anything at all.

MRS. WHITEHEAD. Suppose I were to ask you to take away the Beaugard sculpture, oh just temporarily, and substitute a little thing of my own.

HIVES. I should consider it rather extraordinary.

MRS. WHITEHEAD. It is, Hives. But somehow I still think of you as one of the Whiteheads.

HIVES. Thank you. It's hard for a man to serve two mistresses.

MRS. WHITEHEAD. It's been done. (*takes his arm and starts to walk him toward exit*)

HIVES. My soul is yours, even though my body may belong to Mrs. Rittenhouse.

MRS. WHITEHEAD. Why, Hives.

(*MRS. WHITEHEAD and HIVES exit. Thunder and lightning. RAVELLI enters through French doors carrying statue wrapped under a sheet. There is a loud burst of thunder and lightning as the PROFESSOR enters through French doors carrying a step ladder and several tools.*)

RAVELLI. Hurry up. You want to get wet? Now listen, we got to be very quiet. (*PROFESSOR drops tools and pushes ladder over to the ledge underneath the statue, drops tool bag.*) Somebody come. Hide. (*PROFESSOR stands on his head. RAVELLI hides behind couch.*) Never mind, it's a mistake, nobody come. (*RAVELLI shows PROFESSOR duplicate statue.*) Now listen, we got to take this statue down — (*indicates statue up on ledge*) — and put this one up. (*PROFESSOR caresses statue.*) No touch. (*PROFESSOR slaps his own hand.*) You got everything, the shovel, the axe, the dynamite, the pineapples? Where you got the flash? The flash. The flash. (*PROFESSOR indicates his own flesh by pinching his own cheek.*) No. No. The flash, the flash. (*PROFESSOR takes out fish from pocket.*) That's a fish. I no wanna a fish. Now you act crazy. Flash. When you go out in the night time you gotta have a flash. (*PROFESSOR takes out large silver flask.*) That's a flisk. I no wanna flisk. When you wanna see somebody, you gotta have the flash. (*PROFESSOR takes out five playing cards.*) That's a flush. What do I need a flush for? (*PROFESSOR takes out a spray gun.*) No, that's a flits. I don't want a flits. (*PROFESSOR takes out a flute and plays.*) No flutes. You got flutes, the flits, the flask, the flush . . . (*PROFESSOR plays flute.*) Stop it, you crazy. Now listen to me. When it's light and you wanna make it dark, you gotta have the flash. (*PROFESSOR takes out black-jack.*) That's a black-jack. No, I make a mistake. When it's dark outside and you wanna make a light then you gotta have a flash. (*PROFESSOR finally brings out a flashlight.*) That'sa what I want. I knew you had it in you. (*PROFESSOR flashes light in his own face. Then covers his eyes with his hand.*) Now we getta da statue. (*There is a loud crash of thunder and lightning. ALL STAGE LIGHTS OUT.*) That's fine. The storm put the lights out. Now nobody can see what we do. Where's the flash? Where's the flash? I no wanna the fish. The flash. (*PROFESSOR plays the flute.*) No flutes. Where you got the flash? What's the matter, you lose it? Look for it. (*PROFESSOR lights flash and looks around the stage lifting up parts of the couch, evidently looking for the flash-light that he has in his hand.*) Well, we can't find it. We work without a light. Now we get the statue. (*The PROFESSOR starts up ladder, there is a flash of lightning and thunder.*) Quick, somebody come, hide. (*PROFESSOR gets under sheet with statue. SPALDING and MRS. RITTENHOUSE enter.*)

Mrs. Rittenhouse. Good heavens, the lights are out all over the house. It's so dark, you can't see your hand before your face.

Spalding. Well you wouldn't get much enjoyment out of that. I don't know what you're going to do, but I'm going to take a nap. Leave me a call for three o'clock.

Ravelli. Cuckoo, cuckoo, cuckoo.

Spalding. Make that three-thirty.

Ravelli. Cuck.

Spalding. You certainly get service around here. Mrs. Rittenhouse, did you lose a fish? (*PROFESSOR makes a noise with his horn.*)

Mrs. Rittenhouse. I beg your pardon! Good heavens, there's somebody over there.

Spalding. Nonsense. It's your imagination. The place is just settling, that's all. Is there anybody over there?

Ravelli. I don't see anybody.

Spalding. There you are. If there was anybody over there, he'd see him, wouldn't I? (*PROFESSOR makes a noise with horn.*)

Mrs. Rittenhouse. (*very mysteriously*) What's that?

Spalding. I think you've got roaches. (*PROFESSOR makes noise.*) Yes, you've got roaches all right, and the biggest one has got asthma. (*There is a tremendous burst of lightning and thunder.*) My mistake, you've got elephants. (*Ladder falls, PROFESSOR's legs dangle from under sheet, he lights flash-light.*)

Ravelli. Boooo! Boooo! (*Thunder and lightning. MRS. RITTENHOUSE screams and exits as RAVELLI restores ladder.*

PROFESSOR comes out from sheet with flash under his chin.
MRS. RITTENHOUSE exits in a tizzy, followed by
SPALDING.) Well, that's fine. We got the statue and we no
make one sound, now we got to get out. That'sa some storm, a
real tomata. Somebody come. *Ah, California.*

(*RAVELLI and PROFESSOR exit. HIVES enters from pit cross
to south standing lamp. Thunder and lightning. HIVES
turns lamp off and on. GRACE puts statue up from pit
south, enters from pit, picks up statue and crosses to Vom
3 landing. HIVES and MRS. WHITEHEAD turn off standing lamps. Black out. HIVES lifts GRACE and statue to
platform. When lights come back up, HIVES, exited, and
GRACE and MRS. WHITEHEAD stand beneath the veiled
statue, looking very innocent as SPALDING enters with
MRS. RITTENHOUSE.*)

MRS. RITTENHOUSE. Captain Spalding, how thrilling! And
then . . . and then what happened?
SPALDING. Oh it was nothing at all. I'd rather not discuss it.
MRS. RITTENHOUSE. Oh, but I can't wait to hear the finish, I
must hear it.
SPALDING. Well, there I was in the top of the tree with this
rhinoceros pointing a gun straight at me. . . . (*He kneels down,
points imaginary gun.*)
MRS. RITTENHOUSE. A rhinoceros? Oh, Captain, what did
you do?
SPALDING. What could I do? I had to marry his daughter.
MRS. RITTENHOUSE. Come right in, everybody. Before we
start the musical program, Captain Spalding is going to tell us all
about his trip to Africa. Captain Spalding. (*All applaud.*)
SPALDING. My friends, I am here tonight to tell you about that
great and wonderfully mysterious continent known as Africa.
Africa is God's country and he can have it. We left New York
drunk and early on the fatal morning of February Second. After
6 days on the water and 3 in the boat, we arrived on the coast of
Africa. We at once proceeded 300 miles into the heart of the jungle, where I shot a polar bear, — This bear was 6 feet 7 inches in
his stocking feet, and he had shoes on at the time.
MRS. RITTENHOUSE. But Captain, I thought Polar bears lived
in the frozen north?
SPALDING. Oh you did, did you? Well this one was a rich bear

and could afford to go away for the winter. You takes care of your animals and I'll take care of mine. From the day of our arrival we led an active life. The first morning saw us up at six, breakfasted and back in bed at seven. This was our routine for the first three months. Then we finally got so we were back in bed by six-thirty. One morning I was sitting in front of the cabin when I bagged six tigers . . . This was the biggest lot . . .

MRS. RITTENHOUSE. Oh, Captain Spalding, did you catch six tigers?

SPALDING. I bagged them . . . I bagged them to go away but they hung around all afternoon. They were the most persistent tigers I have ever seen. The principal animals of the African jungle are moose, elks, and Knights of Pithias. The elks live up in the hills and in the spring they come down for their annual convention . . . It is very interesting to watch them come down to the water hole. And you should see them run when they find out it's only a water hole. What they are looking for is an elcohol. One morning I shot an elephant in my pajamas. How he got in my pajamas, I don't know. Then we tried to remove the tusks. The tusks. That's not so easy to say. Tusks. You try it some time. As I say, we tried to remove the tusks. But they were embedded so firmly we couldn't budge them. Of course, in Alabama, the Tuscaloosa, but that is entirely ir-elephant to what I was talking about. We took some pictures of the native girls, but they weren't developed. But we're going back again in a couple of weeks. Now . . . (*applause*)

MRS. RITTENHOUSE. A very enlightening speech, Captain Spalding.

CHANDLER. Three cheers for Captain Spalding. Three Cheers for Captain Spalding. Three cheers for Captain Spalding. Three Cheers for Captain Spalding.

(*PROFESSOR enters with three chairs.*)

MRS. RITTENHOUSE. (*to PROFESSOR*) No one asked for chairs. Put them right where you found them. Go, go on. Go on, get out. (*CHANDLER pushes the PROFESSOR out of the room. PROFESSOR makes face and exits.*)

CHANDLER. Go on, go on, you.

MRS. RITTENHOUSE. And now, friends, Signor Ravelli will oblige us at the piano. Signor Ravelli. (*applause*)

SPALDING. Signor Ravelli's first selection will be "Somewhere My Loves Lies Sleeping" with a male chorus. (*RAVELLI starts to play, counting to himself. As he nears the end of the piece, he gets stuck on the same phrase.*) Say, if you get near an ending, play it.

RAVELLI. I think I went past it.

SPALDING. Well, if it comes around again, jump off.

RAVELLI. I once kept this up for three days. (*SPALDING gets up and heads towards the piano, rolling up his sleeves. RA-VELLI waves him off.*) Wait, I think I got it. (*He finishes the piece.*) I play you one of my own compositions by Victor Herbert.

SPALDING. Make it short.

OH BY JINGO! OH BY GEE!

IN THE LAND OF SAN DOMINGO
LIVED A GIRL CALLED OH BY JINGO
TA DA DA DA DA DA DA DA
UMPA, UMPA, UMPA, UMPA
FROM THE FIELDS AND THE MARSHES
CAME THE OLD AND YOUNG BY GOSHES
THEY ALL SPOKE WITH A DIFF'RENT LINGO
AND EV'RY NIGHT THEY ALL SANG IN THE
PALE MOONLIGHT.
   CHORUS.
OH BY GEE BY GOSH BY GUM BY JUV
OH BY JINGO, WON'T YOU HEAR OUR LOVE
WE WILL BUILD FOR YOU A HUT
YOU WILL BE OUR FAV'RITE NUT
WE'LL HAVE A LOT OF LITTLE OH BY GOLLIES
THEN WE'LL PUT THEM IN THE FOLLIES
BY JINGO SAID, BY GOSH BY GEE
BY JIMINY PLEASE DON'T BOTHER ME
SO THEY ALL WENT AWAY SINGING
OH BY GEE, BY GOSH, BY GUM BY JUV BY JINGO
BY GEE, YOU'RE THE ONLY GIRL FOR ME.

SO LATE THAT NIGHT THEY MADE A RINGLET
OF FIRE IN THE MIDDLE AND STARTED TO SING
AH YAH YAH DA DA DA DA DA DA

UMPA, UMPA, UMPA, UMPA
SPAKE THE CHIEF SAID BY GEE BY GOSH
BY GUM SHE'LL MARRY ME.
HOWDY THERE, BRING HER HERE TO ME.
YAH, YAH, YAH, YAH.

SO THEY SEARCH FOR HER HERE
AND THEY SEARCH FOR HER THERE
OH ME OH BY GEE
SINGING WHERE OH WHERE
CAN OH BY JINGO BE
FOR SHE MARRIED THAT CROONER
BY THE NAME OF JOE
NOW SHE'S TEACHING THE KID TO SING
BO BO BO BO BO
FAR AWAY FROM SAN DOMINGO
DA DA DA DA DA DA DA

OH BY GEE BY GOSH BY GUM BY JUV
OH BY JINGO, WON'T YOU HEAR OUR LOVE
WE WILL BUILD FOR YOU A HUT
YOU WILL BE OUR FAV'RITE NUT
WE'LL HAVE A LOT OF LITTLE OH BY GOLLIES
THEN WE'LL PUT US IN THE FOLLIES
BY JINGO SAID, BY GOSH BY GEE
BY JIMINY PLEASE DON'T BOTHER ME
SO THEY ALL WENT AWAY SINGING
OH BY GEE BY GOSH BY GUM BY GUV BY JINGO
BY GEE YOU'RE THE ONLY GIRL FOR ME
BY GEE YOU'RE THE ONLY GIRL FOR ME
BY GEE YOU'RE THE ONLY GIRL FOR ME.

SPALDING. And now, Mrs. Rittenhouse, I have a big surprise for you. (*chest brought in by BUTLERS*) When I departed from Africa, I was presented with a little gift. And that gift, Mrs. Rittenhouse, I'm going to give to you at a very low figure.

MRS. RITTENHOUSE. Well, what is it Captain. What is it?

SPALDING. It's a match box for an elephant. This magnificent chest — (*indicating his own chest*) No, this magnificent chest — (*indicating MRS. RITTENHOUSE's chest*) No, this magnificent chest — (*indicating gift*) I was probably right the first time. This magnificent chest, which has been handed down from Zulu to Zulu for eight hundred generations, now takes it's place among the treasures of your beautiful home.

RAVELLI. (*reading tag on chest*) Grand Rapids. (*SPALDING immediately tears tag off.*)

MRS. RITTENHOUSE. Captain, this leaves me speechless.

SPALDING. Well, see that you remain that way.

MRS. RITTENHOUSE. And now for the unveiling of the statue, through the graciousness of M. Doucet. (*applause*) It is my privilege to reveal the masterpiece of Francois Jacques Dubois Guilbert Beaugard.

SPALDING. On track twenty-five. No trains will be sold after the magazines leave the depot.

MRS. RITTENHOUSE. "After the Hunt." (*HIVES pulls the veil off.*)

CHORUS. (*exclamation*) Wonderful, Beautiful, etc.

CHANDLER. (*pushing his way through the crowd*) Wait, there must be some mistake. This sculpture is not a "Beaugard".

CHORUS. Mistake! A mistake!

DOUCET. (*forces his way through*) Stop! This statue is a fake. The "Beaugard" is stolen.

CHORUS. A fake? It's a fake.

MRS. WHITEHEAD. That's what I call a pretty rotten break. (*to MRS. RITTENHOUSE*)

DOUCET. This sculpture spurious will drive me furious. This imitation means ruination.

CHORUS. Doucet is furious, this is injurious, this news will cause a big sensation.

WALLY. Now this is scandal that I can handle. I'll get it into the Traffic.

MRS. WHITEHEAD AND GRACE. I wonder how the crime was done and who could be the guilty one.

CHORUS. We'd like to know the guilty one.

SPALDING. Maybe I did it.

ALL. You!

JAMISON. No! The Captain is a moral man, he wouldn't stoop to crooking.

SPALDING. This fact I emphasize with stress, I never steal a thing unless nobody's looking.

OMNES. The Captain is a very moral man.

JOHN. My star's descended, there goes my career. My hopes are ended, my dear.

MARY. We'll survive long as we feel romantic.

CHORUS. Love will thrive as long as you feel romantic. Other folks crumble when they're feeling blue.

JOHN & MARY. But it's easy to feel romantic with you.

SPALDING. It's about time I took a hand in this little affair. Jamison, are the doors locked?

JAMISON. Yes, sir.

SPALDING. Nobody can get in or out?

JAMISON. No, sir.

SPALDING. Well, I'll throw a little light on this subject. (*Blackout. Exclamations from ALL.*)

ALL. The lights. What happened to the lights? Where are the lights? Lights. (*Lights up. The Beaugard is missing.*)

CHANDLER. (*seeing the statue gone*) Look! That one is gone, too. (*shots off stage*) The crooks! They are escaping. Come with me.

(*ALL exit. The lid of the chest slowly opens. The PROFESSOR emerges. He takes the three statues out of the chest. He tries to carry all three statues, cannot. He has an idea. He puts the statues in the chest, pulls out a rope from his coat, attaches it to the chest and tries to pull it off. He can't. Just then a girl enters. The PROFESSOR's face lights up. He grabs the girl and throws her into chest, climbing after her.*)

CURTAIN

ACT TWO

SCENE: *The breakfast room. The next morning.*
AT RISE: *MRS. WHITEHEAD, GRACE and HIVES are discovered.*

MRS. WHITEHEAD. Well?

HIVES. Good morning, Miss Grace. Good morning, my lady.

MRS. WHITEHEAD. Good morning, my eye. Where have you been all night?

HIVES. Oh, I don't know. I hardly know how to tell you.

GUESTS. Tell us what?

HIVES. Mrs. Rittenhouse is in an awful state.

MRS. WHITEHEAD. Good.

HIVES. Monsieur Doucet keeps screaming for the police.

GUESTS. Good.

HIVES. Mr. Chandler is terribly upset about something he read in this morning's paper.

MRS. WHITEHEAD & GRACE. Good.

HIVES. And nobody has their orange juice yet. But to top it all off . . . (*HIVES imitates statue.*)

MRS. WHITEHEAD. The statue?

GUESTS. Which one?

HIVES. Somebody stole the Beaugard from my room.

MRS. WHITEHEAD. Good God.

HIVES. And then when the lights went out, someone hit me over the head and stole Miss Grace's imitation.

MRS. WHITEHEAD. Good God. Then you didn't put out the lights?

GUESTS. Who was it?

HIVES. I don't know, Miss Grace.

GUESTS. Oh, Hives, everything was fixed.

MRS. WHITEHEAD. Wait a minute—when the lights were put on again I happened to notice that there was one person missing—

GUESTS. The Professor.

HIVES. Good God.

MRS. WHITEHEAD. Hives, I feel better all ready. I know exactly what to do.

GUESTS. (*exiting*) Haven't we a couple of nasty dispositions?

MRS. WHITEHEAD. (*exiting with GRACE*) Haven't we though.

(*WINSTON gay and debonair and dressed in bright sports clothes enters whistling. He owns the world. He notices the "Traffic," picks it up, gives it a glance and rubs his hands in enjoyment.*)

WINSTON. Hello, old socks. And how are you this morning?

HIVES. Lousy.

WINSTON. Well I've got a little tonic here that will put you dead to rights. Ever read the "Morning Traffic"?

HIVES. God forbid, sir. Oh, a telegram for you, sir. (*handing him telegram*)

WINSTON. Thank you, Hives. (*opening telegram*) And if this is what I think it is, and I think it is, yes, it is. Here you are, Hives. Take this and buy yourself some laughing soup. (*hands HIVES a bill*)

HIVES. Thank you very much, Sir. (*Exits. ARABELLA entering, sees this.*)

ARABELLA. That's it. Squander your money on Butlers — while I stand over a hot stove.

WINSTON. Baby you can throw away the hot stove — I'm going to buy you a Frigidaire. Drop your mascara on this. (*handing her telegram*)

ARABELLA. (*reading a phrase*) "Your brilliant work in unearthing the Roscoe W. Chandler, item" — A fifty dollar raise. Oh, Wally that's wonderful.

WINSTON. (*glancing at telegram*) A fifty dollar raise. Let me see — is that every week? Yes. Why you are practically Mrs. Wally Winston this minute.

ARABELLA. Oh you're going to do the right thing are you?

WINSTON. I always do the right thing.

ARABELLA. You don't say. How many right things have you ever done?

WINSTON. I take it back. I never did the right thing before in my life.

ARABELLA. I got some bad news for you. Beautiful society queen accepts tabloid dirt disher.

WINSTON. (*embracing her*) Whoopee! That makes it clear sailing.

ARABELLA. Then we're both in the same boat. (*They kiss.*)

HIVES. A telegram, sir. (*WINSTON does not notice him.*) A telegram, sir.

ARABELLA. Wally, a telegram.

HIVES. A telegram for you, sir. (*handing it over*)

ARABELLA. Another raise.

WINSTON. It wouldn't surprise me. (*hands HIVES a bill*) Here you are, Hives. Go out and buy yourself some more laughing soup.

HIVES. Thank you very much, sir. (*exits*)

WINSTON. (*opening telegram*) When luck comes it comes in bunches. It never rains luck but what it pours luck. (*He has scanned the wire — his smile slowly fades away.*)

ARABELLA. What's the matter?

WINSTON. (*looks at the wire from various angles, gives up — hands it to ARABELLA*) What do you think that says?

ARABELLA. (*takes it, looks at it — a pause*) You're fired.

WINSTON. While you were finding out things about Chandler why didn't you find out that he owns the paper? (*weakly*) Chandler is the owner of the paper.

ARABELLA. Yeah —

WINSTON. Did you know that?

ARABELLA. No I didn't.

WINSTON. I didn't either. Silly me. Fired. I can see tomorrow's column now.

ARABELLA. Oh, Wally . . .

WINSTON. Tabloid Dirt Disher Dumped by Debutante. Coupon Clipper Kabbible Cans Columnist for playing in Morning Traffic. Arabella, I'm ruined. I'm washed up. I'm finished. (*He starts to cry, tears up the telegram into small bits as HIVES enters.*)

ARABELLA. Oh, Wally, cheer up. I know you can beat this. You can. Crying won't help.

HIVES. Is anything the matter sir?

WINSTON. (*puts torn telegram on HIVE's salver*) Is anything the matter? Read that! (*continues crying*)

HIVES. (*begins to laugh*) Fired.

ARABELLA. Hives, that's not funny.

HIVES. (*laughing*) Canned.

ARABELLA. Hives.

HIVES. (*laughing*) Sacked. (*HIVES exits.*)

ARABELLA. (*calling after him*) Skunk!

WINSTON. Well, Arabella, I'm afraid this may be my last Rittenhouse party.

ARABELLA. Can you imagine that bimbo Chandler turning out to own the paper?

Winston. Well, I'm not surprised. Just the same, I sure will miss all this. And you.

Arabella. Wally.

Winston. Traffic tipster bids farewell to Long Island Low-down.

Arabella. I still think you're terrific. What is society anyhow, just a bunch of high-brows hobnobbing at a speakeasy with no cover charge.

Winston. It's more than that, Arabella, take a tip from me.

(*Sings: LONG ISLAND LOWDOWN*)

Wally.
WHEN YOU ARE INVITED OUT AMONG THE WHO IS
    WHO.
YOU'LL HEAR THE BAND BEGIN TO PLAY A MELODY
    BLUE;
YOU'LL SEE THEM DO A DANCE
AND YOU MUST LEARN IT TO BE IN THE SWIM
THEN EV'RY ONE DANCES TILL
THE SUN COMES PEEPING THROUGH
AND STARS GROW DIM.
(*Refrain*)
FOLLOW THE STYLE
AND DO THE LONG ISLAND LOW DOWN, LOW DOWN.
TAKE OFF YOUR SPATS AND THROWN YOUR HIGH
    HATS AWAY
LEARN HOW TO TAP YOUR HIP
WHILE YOU SLAP YOUR TOE DOWN, TOE DOWN.
COME FROM BELOW
GET IN TO THE SOCIAL SWAY.
YOU SHOULD SEE THE FEET START TO FLY
WHEN ALL THE HIGH BROWS GET HOT.
THAT UPPER CRUST KICKS UP A DUST AND HOW
FOLLOW THE STYLE
AND DO THE LONG ISLAND LOW DOWN, LOW DOWN.
PEOPLE HIGH UP
ARE DOING THE LOW DOWN NOW.
    Chorus.
WHEN YOU ARE INVITED OUT AMONG THE WHO IS
    WHO
YOU'LL HEAR THE BAND BEGIN TO PLAY A MELODY
    BLUE

YOU'LL SEE THEM DO A DANCE
AND YOU MUST LEARN IT TO BE IN THE SWIM
THEN EV'RYONE DANCES
TILL THE SUN COMES PEEPING THROUGH
AND STARS GROW DIM.
WALLY.
FOLLOW THE STYLE
AND DO THE LONG ISLAND LOW DOWN, LOW DOWN.
TAKE OFF YOUR SPATS AND THROW YOUR HIGH
  HATS AWAY.
LEARN HOW TO TAP YOUR HIP
WHILE YOU SLAP YOUR TOE DOWN, TOE DOWN.
COME FROM BELOW
GET INTO THE SOCIAL SWAY.
CHORUS.
FOLLOW THE STYLE
AND DO THE LONG ISLAND LOW DOWN, LOW DOWN.
PEOPLE HIGH UP ARE
DOING THE LOW DOWN NOW.

(*MRS. RITTENHOUSE enters. WINSTON, ARABELLA and CHORUS exit. JAMISON enters.*)

MRS. RITTENHOUSE. Good morning, Mr. Jamison. And how is Captain Spalding this morning?
JAMISON. Oh, he had a very bad night. We went horse-back riding in the middle of the night.
MRS. RITTENHOUSE. I'm so sorry. But of course we've all been pretty well upset.

(*CAPTAIN SPALDING enters. He is wearing a riding costume. He begins looking around the room for something he has obviously lost.*)

MRS. RITTENHOUSE. (*continued*) Good morning, Captain Spalding. Did you enjoy your ride? What in the world are you looking for?
SPALDING. I lost my horse. He slipped right out from between me.
MRS. RITTENHOUSE. Oh, that's too bad, Captain Spalding. But don't worry—
SPALDING. Don't worry? I suppose you could go horse-back riding without a horse. I even lost the bit you loaned me.

MRS. RITTENHOUSE. Oh, that's all right. I'll give you another bit.

SPALDING. Then that'll be two bits I owe you.

MRS. RITTENHOUSE. Captain I hope that you've not been too distressed by last night's unfortunate occurrence.

SPALDING. You mean the dinner you served?

MRS. RITTENHOUSE. No, no — I mean the statue that was stolen.

SPALDING. You ought to scour the whole place. It probably needs it too. Jamison, why didn't you tell me there was a statue stolen? What do you think I hired you for?

JAMISON. Why Captain, I didn't know it.

SPALDING. You should have asked me. I didn't know it either.

JAMISON. Well, I'm sorry.

SPALDING. You're sorry, you're a contemptible cur. I repeat, Sir, you're a contemptible cur. Oh, if I were a man, you'd resent that. (*to MRS. RITTENHOUSE*) Please keep quiet, will ya? (*to JAMISON*) I can get along without you, you know. I got along without your father, didn't I? Yes, and your grandfather, yes, and your uncle. (*to MRS. RITTENHOUSE*) Yes, and *your* uncle. Yes, and my uncle.

MRS. RITTENHOUSE. But Captain . . .

SPALDING. I didn't come here to be distributed. (*HIVES enters.*)

HIVES. I beg your pardon, Mrs. Rittenhouse.

SPALDING. (*to HIVES*) Yes — and your uncle.

HIVES. I beg your pardon, Mrs. Rittenhouse, the police are on their way.

MRS. RITTENHOUSE. The police? Have them come in when they arrive. (*HIVES bows and exits.*)

SPALDING. Oh, so that's your game, is it? Well they can't shut me up.

MRS. RITTENHOUSE. But Captain —

SPALDING. No, no you can talk to my attorney. Jamison, take a letter to my lawyer. (*JAMISON sits in chair right of table. Takes out note-book and pencil. MRS. RITTENHOUSE stands behind table right.*) I'll show you a thing or two or three. Jamison, take dictation.

MRS. RITTENHOUSE. Oh, Captain!

JAMISON. I'm taking it.

SPALDING. I'll show you a thing or three. Begin this way, Jamison. Let's get off with a bang. "Hon. Charles D. Hungerdunger, c/o Hungerdunger — Hungerdunger and McCormick. Gentlemen, question-mark. In re yours of the fifth inst. yours to hand and in reply, I wish to state that the judiciary expenditures of this year, i.e. has not exceeded the fiscal year — brackets — this procedure is problematic and with nulification will give us a subsidiary indictment and priority. Quotes, unquotes, and quotes. Hoping this finds you, ahem, I beg to remain. . . .

JAMISON. Do you want that "ahem" in the letter?

SPALDING. No put that in an envelope. Hoping this finds you, I beg to remain as of June the 9th, cordially respectfully regards. That's all Jamison. (*to MRS. RITTENHOUSE*) I'll show you where I get off. Sending for the police. (*to JAMISON*) Now read what you have Jamison.

JAMISON. (*reading*) Hon. Charles D. Hungerdunger, . . .

SPALDING. Hunga dunga.

BOTH. Hunga. . . . Hunga

JAMISON. Hungadunga.

SPALDING. That's it. Hungerdunger.

JAMISON. C/O Hungerdunger-Hungerdunger and McCormick . . .

SPALDING. You left out a Hungerdunger. You left out the main one. Thought you could slip one over on me, didn't you, eh? Alright, leave it out and put in a windshield wiper instead. No, make that three windshield wipers and one Hungerdunger. They all won't be there when the letter arrives anyhow.

JAMISON. (*reading*) Gentlemen, question mark . . .

SPALDING. Gentlemen questionmark . . . put it on the dip-thong, not on the penultimate.

JAMISON. (*reading*) In re yours of the fifth, inst . . . Now you said a lot of things here that I didn't think were important, so I just omitted them.

SPALDING. So, you just omitted them, eh?

MRS. RITTENHOUSE. Oh Captain. Good Gracious. Oh my.

SPALDING. (*business with the crop*) You just omitted them, eh? You left out the body of the letter. Yours not to reason why, you left out the body of the letter. Alright, send it that way, and tell them the body will follow. Closely followed by yours.

JAMISON. Want the body in brackets?

SPALDING. No, it'll never get there in brackets. Put it in a box, put it in a box and mark it F-r-a-g-i-l-e-.

JAMISON. Mark it what?

SPALDING. Mark it Fragile F-r-a-g------look it up, Jamison. Look under Fragile.

JAMISON. (*reading*) Quotes, unquotes and quotes.

Spalding. That's three quotes?
Jamison. Yes, sir.
Spalding. Add another quote and make it a gallon. How much is a gallon?
Jamison. (*reading*) Regards.
Spalding. Jamison, that's an epic. That's fine. That's going to make a dandy letter. That's all. You may go, Jamison. I may go, too.

(*Two POLICEMEN enter.*)

First Policeman. Mrs. Rittenhouse?
Mrs. Rittenhouse. Yes?
First Policeman. I'm Sargeant Hennessey from Headquarters.
Mrs. Rittenhouse. How do you do?
Spalding. Let me introduce myself. I'm Captain Scotland of Spalding yard.
Mrs. Rittenhouse. Mr. Jamison, please show these men to the scene of the crime.
Jamison. Certainly, Mrs. Rittenhouse. Right this way, gentlemen.
Spalding. Jamison! Count the spoons. (*JAMISON and two POLICEMEN exit.*)
Mrs. Rittenhouse. Oh, Captain, I didn't know you were a detective too.
Spalding. There's a lot you don't know.
Mrs. Rittenhouse. I suppose that is so.
Spalding. You're darn right it's so. Where were you on the night of June 5th, 1774?
Mrs. Rittenhouse. I'm afraid I don't know.
Spalding. Why should you? Where was I?
Mrs. Rittenhouse. How should I know?
Spalding. How should you know? If I did, why should I tell you? Take a number from one to ten.
Mrs. Rittenhouse. All right.
Spalding. Alright, what's the number.
Mrs. Rittenhouse. Seven.
Spalding. That's right. Seven is right. I could have done it with one hand if I wanted to. Some mystery, huh! I could solve this in five minutes if I wanted to worry.
Mrs. Rittenhouse. Captain, please don't worry. I don't want anything to interfere with your week-end.

SPALDING. Nothing ever interferes with my week-end and I'll thank you not to get personal, Mrs. Rittenrotten.

MRS. RITTENHOUSE. Oh, please, Captain, you misunderstand me . . . I don't mean it that way . . .

SPALDING. A more dastardly crack I've never heard.

MRS. RITTENHOUSE. Oh, Captain.

SPALDING. I wish I were back in the jungle where men are monkeys.

MRS. RITTENHOUSE. Captain, I'm so sorry, I didn't mean to offend you. . . .

SPALDING. No . . . no . . . no . . . no . . .

(*Sings SHOW ME A ROSE*)

SHOW ME A ROSE I'LL SHOW YOU A GIRL WHO CARES
SHOW ME A ROSE OR LEAVE ME ALONE
SHOW ME A ROSE I'LL SHOW YOU A STAG AT BAY
SHOW ME A ROSE OR LEAVE ME ALONE.

SHE TAUGHT ME HOW TO DO THE TANGO,
DOWN WHERE THE PALM TREES SWAY.
I CALLED HER ROSE MIA, AND SHE CALLED A
SPADE A SPADE.

SHOW ME A ROSE I'LL SHOW YOU A STORM AT SEA
SHOW ME A ROSE OR LEAVE ME ALONE.

ONE NIGHT IN BIXBY ARIZONA, WE WATCHED THE
  CLOUDS ROLL BY
HE SAID MY DEAR HOW ARE YOU AND SHE
  WHISPERED
SO AM I.

SHOW ME A ROSE I'LL SHOW YOU A GIRL NAMED
  SAM,
SHOW ME A ROSE OR LEAVE ME ALONE.
SHOW ME A ROSE A FRAGRANT ROSE.
MAKE ME BELIEVE THAT YOU DON'T KNOW ME
UNTIL YOU SHOW ME A ROSE.

(*enter MRS. WHITEHEAD.*)

MRS. WHITEHEAD. I beg your pardon, am I intruding?

SPALDING. What a question. Are you intruding? I should say you are. Just when I had her on the five yard line. I should say you are intruding. Pardon me I was using the subjunctive instead of the past tense. Yes, we're way past tents. We're living in bungalows now. This is a mechanical age of course.

MRS. RITTENHOUSE. Mrs. Whitehead, you haven't met Captain Spalding, have you?

MRS. WHITEHEAD. Why no, I haven't. We haven't seen much of the Captain, lately, Mrs. Rittenhouse. I am afraid you're being just a little bit selfish.

SPALDING. That's what I was telling her. (*to MRS. WHITEHEAD*) I haven't seen much of you, lately either. And how are you?

MRS. WHITEHEAD. Fine, thank you. And how are you?

SPALDING. And how are you? That leaves you one up. Did anyone ever tell you you had beautiful eyes? Oh yes you have. (*to MRS. RITTENHOUSE*) And so've you. I don't think I've ever seen four more beautiful eyes in my life—three anyway. You know you two women have everything. You're tall and short—and slim and stout—and blonde and brunette—and that's just the kind of a girl I crave. We three would make an ideal couple. You've got beauty, charm, money—you do have money, haven't you? Because if you haven't we can quit right now. My time is not what it used to be.

MRS. WHITEHEAD. (*to MRS. RITTENHOUSE*) The Captain is charming, isn't he?

MRS. RITTENHOUSE. I'm fascinated.

SPALDING. I'm fascinated too—right here on the arm. Oh I'm just an old pleasure man, that's all. If I were Eugene O'Neill I could tell you what I really think of you. You're lucky the Theater Guild isn't putting this on. So is the Guild. Pardon me, while I have a strange interlude. (*He strikes a frozen pose.*) Why you couple of baboons—what makes you think I'd marry either one of you. How strange the wind blows tonight. It has a thin eery voice. Reminds me of poor old Marsden. How happy I could be with either of them if both of them went away. (*to the wind*) Well, what do you say, girls, will you marry me?

MRS. RITTENHOUSE. But Captain, which one of us?

SPALDING. Both of you. Let's all get married. This is my party. (*He strikes a pose.*)—Party—here I am talking of parties—I came down here for a party. What happens? Nothing. Not even ice cream. They show me a statue. They don't even show it to me — they steal it. The Gods look down and laugh. This would be a better world for children if the parents had to eat the spinach. (*to women*) Well, what do you say — are we all going to get married?

MRS. WHITEHEAD. All of us?

SPALDING. All of us.

MRS. WHITEHEAD. But that's bigamy.

SPALDING. Yes — and it's big o' me too. It's big of all of us. Let's be big for a change. I'm sick of these conventional marriages. One woman and one man was good enough for your grandmother — but who wants to marry your grandmother — nobody — not even your grandfather. (*to ladies*) Just think of the honeymoon — strictly private: I wouldn't let another woman in on this. Well, maybe one or two — but no men. I may not even go myself.

MRS. RITTENHOUSE. Are you suggesting Companionate Marriage?

SPALDING. Well, it's got it's advantages. You could live with your folks and I could live with your folks. (*to MRS. WHITE-HEAD*) And you could sell Fuller brushes. (*Pose; music under.*) Living with your folks — the beginning of the end — drab dead yesterdays shutting out the beautiful tomorrows — hideous stumbling footsteps — creaking along the misty corridors of time — time — time. You may not believe it, but they used to give Pulitzer prizes for this stuff. Let's see where was I? Oh yes, we were about to get married. Well, what do you think. Do you think we ought to get married? (*All start toward entrance.*)

MRS. RITTENHOUSE. I think marriage is a very noble institution.

MRS. WHITEHEAD. It's the foundation of the American home.

SPALDING. But the trouble is you can't enforce it. It was put over on the American people while our boys were over there.

(*Music. Two BUTLERS enter, strike North and South tables and chairs exit. As DOUCET enters and POLICE enter.*)

DOUCET. Allez, allez. We have searched this room. The statue is not here. Follow me Allons.

SPALDING. I guess it's time to follow the plot girls. (*MRS. RITTENHOUSE and MRS. WHITEHEAD split.*) No, I'll follow you instead. No you. (*to DOUCET*) No you. Not you?

(*Two POLICE exit as DOUCET exits. They stop. One POLICE-MAN crosses after one BUTLER and one POLICEMAN crosses after one BUTLER.*)

DOUCET. No, no, no nin com poops, this way. (*DOUCET crosses as GIRL enters screaming, followed by PROFESSOR.*)

DOUCET. Sacre Bleu! (*DOUCET exits. GIRL crosses North. SPALDING tags PROFESSOR.*)

SPALDING. Now you're it. (*RAVELLI enters. SPALDING crosses North after GIRL. CHANDLER enters. PROFESSOR tags CHANDLER.*)

CHANDLER. Why, it's you two crooks. (*PROFESSOR tags RAVELLI, RAVELLI tags him back. PROFESSOR runs to CHANDLER. RAVELLI sees CHANDLER tags him. CHANDLER goes for RAVELLI then PROFESSOR. RAVELLI runs, PROFESSOR runs.*)

PROFESSOR/RAVELLI. Abie the fish man, Abie the fish man. (*PROFESSOR and RAVELLI exit. Two BUTLERS cross to East and West tables and chairs. Two POLICEMEN follow BUTLERS as DOUCET enters.*)

DOUCET. Allez, allez, follow moi. (*CHANDLER turns to leave as WINSTON and ARABELLA enter, they see each other at disk.*)

CHANDLER. You Winston swine. Come back here.

(*WINSTON and ARABELLA turn and exit, CHANDLER follows them off. POLICE and DOUCET exit. BUTLERS strike tables and chairs. Stage is clear. Trunk comes up on elevator. PROFESSOR creeps up pit steps. PROFESSOR cautiously opens the chest. Out comes the GIRL whom he has secreted the night before. Now, however, she is wearing a negligee. She stamps her foot in vexation and exits. PROFESSOR decides to hide statue under step ramps. MRS. WHITEHEAD enters with GRACE, observing this. PROFESSOR checks chest for third statue, sees MRS. WHITEHEAD and GRACE. Closes chest and sits on it.*)

MRS. WHITEHEAD. I'll engage him in conversation. You two trail behind. (*to PROFESSOR*) Hello. (*leg business*) Don't do that. You know what I want—(*Business. Both sit on chair. PROFESSOR places the statues under him.*) Don't you like me?

(*shakes his head "no"*) Well I like you I like little boys like you. By the way, how old are you? (*PROFESSOR indicates that he is five years old.*) Five years old? Why you're just a baby. (*They both laugh. MRS. WHITEHEAD tries to take one of the statues. The PROFESSOR prevents her.*) Tell me isn't there somebody you love? (*PROFESSOR shakes his head "no".*) Isn't there somebody you're thinking of? (*business*) Tell me—who? (*PRO-FESSOR takes a photograph from pocket, hands it to MRS. WHITEHEAD. She looks at it.*) Why that's a horse.

(*Business with kissing hand and breaking her arm. HIVES enters with bottle of chloroform; business with bottle; knocks out the PROFESSOR. MRS. WHITEHEAD and HIVES retrieve two statues and exit. MARY enters, sees PROFESSOR asleep on chest, cradling chloroform bottle.*)

MARY. Professor! Professor! (*Sleepily, he proffers the bottle.*) Professor, I want to talk to you. (*He sits up.*) Professor, wake up . . . I want to talk to you about the statue . . . I want to thank you for everything you've done, but it's all over now. The joke is over—I want you to put the statue back. (*JOHN enters.*)

JOHN. Mary, where . . .

MARY. Do you understand? I want you to put back the original and give me the other one.

JOHN. Give me the other one. I want to see if it's as bad as they say. (*The PROFESSOR rises from the couch; starts uncertainly toward the chest. Remembers, before he gets to it, that the statues aren't in there any more. Starts back to couch; remembers that everything isn't just right over there, either. Hesitates.*) What's the matter?

MARY. You've got them, haven't you? (*PROFESSOR thinks a moment—alarm goes off. PROFESSOR removes hat. Clock strapped to his head.*) What is it?

JOHN. Haven't you got them? (*Frantic, the PROFESSOR checks chest, discovers statues missing. Goes crazy, runs around. Bell (from orchestra). He takes bottle of chloroform out, sniffs it, sniffs air, sniffs again, takes drink, drops to hands and knees, exits sniffing. JOHN goes to chest.*) Here we are! (*reaches in, brings out third statue*)

MARY. Thank God! (*They both look at the statue as JOHN uncovers it.*)

JOHN. Mary! Look!

MARY. What's the matter?

JOHN. This isn't mine—and it isn't the Beaugard either.

MARY. A third one? I don't understand.

JOHN. (*thoughtfully looking at the statue*) Wait a minute— somebody else had the same brilliant notion that you did—don't you see?

MARY. All I know is—that the musicians took the Beaugard and put yours in its place.

JOHN. And then somebody stole mine thinking it was the Beaugard. And this is what they left us. Say, they certainly got the better of the bargain, all right. This is pretty awful. I know I'm better than this anyhow.

MARY. Better than this? Why, you're better than Beaugard.

JOHN. I know dear.

MARY. (*kisses him, gently*) I know. This gives us new courage.

JOHN. But it doesn't give us the Beaugard. Don't forget we've still got a couple of clouds hanging over us.

MARY. Let 'em hang! They can't rain on our party.

WATCHING THE CLOUDS ROLL BY

JOHN.
NEARLY EV'RY NEW DAY
FOR ME WAS A BLUE DAY
MY LIFE WAS JUST ONE BLUE MONDAY
HOW THE DAYS WOULD DRAG ON
IF THEY HAD NO TAG ON
I COULDN'T TELL WHICH WAS SUNDAY
I KEPT MY EYES ON
THE HORIZON, BUT ONLY CLOUDS WERE THERE
NOTHING COULD MOVE THEM, NOBODY SEEMED
    TO CARE,
SUDDENLY YOU STEPPED IN
AND HAPPINESS CREPT IN
AND EVERYTHING CHANGED IN ONE DAY
NOW YOU AND I
CAN CLEAR THE SKY
CHORUS.
LOOKING FOR THE SUN.
TWO LOVING HEARTS ARE BETTER THAN ONE

WE'LL HAVE LOTS OF FUN
WATCHING THE CLOUDS ROLL BY.
CARES DON'T MEAN A THING
WHETHER IT'S WINTER, WHETHER IT'S SPRING
WHILE TWO HEARTS CAN SING,
WATCHING THE CLOUDS ROLL BY.
WE'LL BE AS NEAR LIKE LOVE BIRDS
AS ANY TWO,
AND DEAR IF WE'RE LIKE LOVE BIRDS
WHAT ARE A FEW APRIL SHOWERS
WHEN IT'S DARK OR FAIR
WHAT DOES IT MATTER, WHAT DO WE CARE
IF WE BOTH ARE THERE
WATCHING THE CLOUDS ROLL BY.

MARY. (*as number ends*) Quick, take this statue and lock it in your room. I'll try and find Captain Spalding. I know he will help. (*SPALDING pops up through trap.*)

SPALDING. Did someone say Spalding? I couldn't help overhearing, and I must say I find your predicament very interesting. Well—fairly interesting, anyhow. But don't worry, little girl, I'll buy your flowers. No—it was a statue, wasn't it?

MARY. But Captain, I feel so guilty. If it hadn't been for me, maybe the statue would never have been stolen.

SPALDING. Now, don't worry everything's going to be alright. You let me work on this case for twenty-four hours and then we'll call in somebody else. You think it's a mystery now—wait till you see it tomorrow. Remember the Charley Ross disappearance? I worked on that for twenty-four hours and they never did find him. They couldn't find me for five years.

JOHN. Say, you know if we could find the person that sculpted this we'd have a pretty good clue.

SPALDING. Let's see it. Ah, ah, it's signed, Beaugard. There's the criminal, Beaugard.

JOHN. No—Beaugard is dead.

SPALDING. Beaugard is dead? Then it's murder. (*Enter RAVELLI.*) Now, we've got something.

RAVELLI. What have you got?

SPALDING. I've got Jacks and Eights. What've you got?

RAVELLI. Good! I was bluffing.

SPALDING. (*has been regarding the statue*) Look at this—isn't there something that strikes you very funny about this?

RAVELLI. (*laughing heartily*) That'sa funny.

SPALDING. Come, come—it's not as funny as that. Do you

know what this is? This is a left-handed sculpture. Here, John, take this and hide it where no man has ever set foot . . . try Mrs. Rittenhouse's bedroom. (*JOHN and MARY exit. SPALDING pacing the floor.*) Ravelli, we have to find the left handed sculpter. In a case like this, the first thing you've got to do is find the motive. Find the motive and you've got the motive. Now what could've been the motive of the guys that swiped the Beaugard?

RAVELLI. (*after considerable thought*) I got it. Robbery.

SPALDING. You know, sometimes I think it would have been better if your mother had remained single.

RAVELLI. Hey, Cap, it come to me like a flash. This statue wasn't stolen. This statue it disappear. What make this statue disappear? Moths. Moths eat it. Left handed moths.

SPALDING. Left handed moths ate the statue. You know, I'd buy you a parachute if I thought it wouldn't open.

RAVELLI. (*pointing to his shoes*) I got a pair of shoes.

SPALDING. (*climbs on table and groans*) Come on, let's go down and get the reward. We solved it. You solved it. The statue was eaten by a left handed moth. The credit is all yours.

RAVELLI. Say, you know we did a good days work.

SPALDING. How do you feel, tired? Maybe you ought to lie down for a couple of years. Why don't you lie down until rigor mortis sets in.

RAVELLI. No, I stick it out.

SPALDING. Say, I'll tell you how we can get this statue. We'll go to court and we'll get a writ of habeas corpus.

RAVELLI. Get rid of what?

SPALDING. Well, I walked right into that one. Habeas corpus. Didn't you ever see a habeas corpus?

RAVELLI. No, but I see "Habee's Irish Rose".

SPALDING. (*referring to audience*) Be careful, I think they're armed.

(*RAVELLI and SPALDING pull out guns on audience as elevator takes them down. Enter DOUCET, excitedly, followed by HIVES, POLICEMEN with JOHN in custody, MARY follows. JOHN is carrying the statue.*)

DOUCET. Madame, madame.

MRS. RITTENHOUSE. The statue. Thank God.

DOUCET. No, not the Beaugard—the imitation. But where do you think I find it? In the room occupied by the young man Monsieur what is his name? The police find it in his room.

HIVES. In Mr. Parker's room, madam.

MRS. RITTENHOUSE. (*turning to JOHN*) Mr. Parker?

DOUCET. (*shakes statue under JOHN's nose*) We find this imitation in your room. What have you done with my Beaugard?

CHANDLER. Well, speak. What have you done with it?

DOUCET. Yes.

MARY. Oh, John!

JOHN. There's nothing I can say. I didn't steal it.

DOUCET. Sacre bleu. Where is my Beaugard?

CHANDLER. What do you mean you didn't steal it?

MRS. RITTENHOUSE. Really I think it would be wise of you.

JOHN. I have nothing to say, except that I did not steal the Beaugard.

MARY. I'm the one you can arrest.

JOHN. No, Mary. If you think I stole it, arrest me.

DOUCET. We arrest you—we turn both of you over to the police.

(*Song "OLD KENTUCKY HOME" is being sung off-stage. Just before the end of it in time to sing the last notes on stage, there enters SPALDING, JAMISON, RAVELLI and the PROFESSOR; ALL are in bathing suits. There is a second of harmonizing—arms about each other's shoulders.*)

SPALDING. This program is being broadcast through the courtesy of the Battle Creek Sanitarium. (*The PROFESSOR wearing a bathing suit upside down, comes from behind some of the guests.*) He's either got that thing on upside down or I'm standing on my hands.

MARY. Captain what are we going to do? They're going to arrest us—they found the sculpture in John's room.

SPALDING. Who's going to arrest you?

DOUCET. Moi.

MRS. RITTENHOUSE. I'm sorry to say that it looks pretty bad for them.

SPALDING. Nonsense. In a case like this it's never the first person suspected. You're old enough to know that. You're older.

DOUCET. I demand that these two be placed under arrest.

CHANDLER. By all means—or nobody will be safe here.

SPALDING. What? Those two? Why, you can't arrest them. That's the hero and the heroine. I'm surprised at you, Mr.

Chandler. You wouldn't eat green apples, would you. Not if you had my stomach you wouldn't.

Doucet. I demand that the statue be returned this minute or they be placed under arrest. Do you understand? I demand that the police be called. This instant! I demand, that they be put in jail. I demand—(*The PROFESSOR, who has been sneaking up behind DOUCET, has poured liquid into spray pump and sprays in DOUCET's face. Growing weaker, DOUCET continues.*) I demand that they be arrested. I demand—(*He drops.*)

Mrs. Rittenhouse. Why, what's the matter?

Mrs. Whitehead. He's fainted!

Chandler. Somebody get a doctor.

Grace. Good heavens! (*They are all crowding around the fallen form. As they do so, the PROFESSOR applies the handkerchief to CHANDLER, and he topples over.*)

Mrs. Rittenhouse. Good heavens! Now Mr. Chandler has fainted!

Mrs. Whitehead. What?

Grace. It must be the air!

Spalding. (*By way of helping the PROFESSOR, indicates MRS. WHITEHEAD as the next victim.*) That one there. (*She topples over.*) I never did like her.

Ravelli. Give me some. I help.

(*The PROFESSOR passes on to GRACE; puts her out. Then administers to the various BOYS and GIRLS who are crowding around. As the last one topples over, he waves to JOHN and MARY, indicating that they should make their escape. They exit. The stage is strewn with bodies, left standing are SPALDING, JAMISON, RAVELLI and the PROFESSOR.*)

Spalding. We will now attempt to saw a woman in half.

Jamison. (*who has been listening near the door*) Sssh! Somebody's coming.

Ravelli. The police. (*Now the PROFESSOR sprays JAMISON, RAVELLI and SPALDING. Each of them falls in protest.*)

Spalding. (*as he falls*) Oh, so young, so young.

(*PROFESSOR sprays himself and curls up with the statue.*

HIVES enters, studies the array of bodies, then solemnly announces:)

HIVES. Dinner is served.

SCENE 2

SCENE: *The Professor's dream. To the strains of harp music, the sleeping guests rise, and dreamily gather around the elevator opening. Elevator rises carrying THE PROFESSOR and his harp. The guests exit and PROFESSOR dances a pas de deux with the HARP GIRL — the headpiece of the harp having come to life.*

SCENE 3

SCENE: *The garden, that night. A french garden of the period of Louis XV. BALLET. After the Ballet, HIVES, as the Major Domo, enters.*)

HIVES. Monsieurs et Madames, Her Majesty, The Queen. (*MRS. RITTENHOUSE enters escorted by four ladies-in-waiting.*)
MRS. RITTENHOUSE. We thank the citizens of Burgundy for their gracious tributes on this our birthday and in recognition thereof you are invited to attend the Royal festivities. Let the pageant begin.
HIVES. His majesty, the King.

(*JAMISON enters dressed as a Musketeer. Other attendants enter and stand at attention. SPALDING enters as the King. Exit HIVES.*)

SPALDING. Is this the palace?
JAMISON. Yes sire.
SPALDING. I always wanted to play the Palace. . . . And I'm the king?
JAMISON. Yes sire.
SPALDING. Well France is in a hell of a fix. (*Attendants exit*

through screen doors—SPALDING stands watching after them.)

JAMISON. Sire, the Queen presents her compliments to your Majesty, and begs that you will attend the musicale to be given in her honor. Mr. Jean Beaugard will present her Royal Highness with his latest sculpture.

SPALDING. You give the Queen my compliments and tell her to lay off the razor blades. She'll understand. (*Exit JAMISON. Enter RAVELLI.*)

RAVELLI. Hey King!

SPALDING. Hey King? Mr. King to you.

RAVELLI. I've got to speak to you a minute.

SPALDING. What's up?

RAVELLI. Madame DuBarry is downstairs.

SPALDING. DuBarry is downstairs?

RAVELLI. In a taxi.

SPALDING. Is the meter running? Where's her husband?

RAVELLI. Pittsburgh.

SPALDING. You're sure this time? You know it doesn't look right for a King to jump out of a window at three o'clock in the morning. The last window I jumped out of I forgot to open. I'd show you the scars—but I know you don't smoke. I'll tell you what; Tell her to come on up. I'll let her do the jumping this time. (*Exit RAVELLI.*) Jamison. Now listen I've got a little affair of State to attend to, and I don't want the Queen horning in. Get me? You keep her out of here and there's a nickel in it for you.

JAMISON. Yes, Sire. (*There is a knock at the door.*)

SPALDING. Filet mignon. (*Enter MRS. WHITEHEAD as DuBarry.*)

MRS. WHITEHEAD. (*after a stately curtsey*) Your Majesty.

SPALDING. DuBarry.

MRS. WHITEHEAD. Sire, I fear for me to come here is indiscreet.

SPALDING. Nonsense. You'd be in the street sooner or later. DuBarry, you look wonderful in that French dressing. (*They both sit at table.*) How about a nice little drink?

MRS. WHITEHEAD. Fine.

SPALDING. Garcon! (*Enter JAMISON.*) Bring some of that very old champagne. Right off the boat.

JAMISON. Yes, sire. (*Exit JAMISON.*)

SPALDING. Pardon me, do you drink?

MRS. WHITEHEAD. If your Majesty wishes.

SPALDING. Your damn-tootin' his Majesty wishes. Why do you think I got you up here for? To show you my magic lantern? Well, we'll slide over that. By the way, may I call you Dudu?

MRS. WHITEHEAD. As you will, mi-lord.

SPALDING. (*Business of SPALDING rubbing a log of the table, as JAMISON enters with champagne.*) Well, pour yourself a good stiff shot, Du—and don't forget your old Louis. (*There is a knock at the door.*)

SPALDING. We're raided. Tell them you're the engineer. (*RA-VELLI and PROFESSOR enter. They are dressed as musketeers.*) Who goes there—friend or foe?

RAVELLI. One of each.

SPALDING. Just as I thought, a pair of french heels. Advance friend and greet your Majesty. (*The PROFESSOR embraces the KING at the same time taking a bottle of champagne from the table. The PROFESSOR and RAVELLI start to exit.*) That was a swell bottle of wine we almost had.

MRS. WHITEHEAD. What does it matter, sire? We have each other, haven't we?

SPALDING. Well you have me there—and I have you here. And that reminds me—Call me Louis, not because its me, just because I want you to call me Louis. (*He starts to embrace her. RAVELLI enters with a sandwich in his hand.*)

RAVELLI. Got any mustard, Louis?

SPALDING. Look in the library.

RAVELLI. Where is the library?

SPALDING. Fifth Avenue and Forty-second street. (*RAVELLI nods and exits, shouting "Taxi".*) Well let's see where were we? Oh yes, I had you there—(*He sits on DuBarry's lap.*) Well that's neither here nor there. (*Girl enters and exits, followed by PRO-FESSOR. On his way out the PROFESSOR stops at the table and exchanges an empty bottle for a full one; starts to exit.*) Say just a minute—you've got a nickel coming for the empty bottle. (*PROFESSOR exits.*)

MRS. WHITEHEAD. Your Majesty has but to command, sire— the King can do no wrong.

SPALDING. You bet I can't. Not with all these interruptions I can't. (*They both sit on couch.*) Ah, it's good to be alone. That's no time to be good, though. Anyhow, we're alone. (*RAVELLI enters.*) My mistake.

RAVELLI. Hey, I can't find the mustard.

SPALDING. You don't think I'm trying to hide it from you, do you?

RAVELLI. My partner. Maybe he's got it. You seen him?

SPALDING. He's due along here any minute now. He runs on the hour and half hour.

RAVELLI. I wait. Move over.

JAMISON. Check, Sire.

SPALDING. Check? $350.60. That's an outrage. (*PROFESSOR and girl enter. Girl exits.*) Roast terrapin $50.00. Baked squab $1.25. Changing one rear tire and five gallons of gas $1200.00 — Say, you forgot to charge me for the wine.

JAMISON. That was on the house, sire.

RAVELLI. Hey, I found the mustard.

SPALDING. I told you you didn't look hard enough. (*SPALDING turns to see DuBarry between RAVELLI and PROFESSOR.*) Oh, so that's your game, is it? You're going to outnumber me are you? Who's girl do you think DuBarry is? You boys better read up on your history.

RAVELLI. You read history, we make it.

SPALDING. You're the King's Musketeer's aren't you?

RAVELLI. Sure.

SPALDING. Attention! About face. (*DuBarry is trying to rise.*) DuBarry, where are you going?

RAVELLI. Oh, you not leave!

(*They all start toward her to pull her back. SPALDING is there first and takes her cape. RAVELLI pulls off part of her dress; the PROFESSOR takes the rest of it. She stands in negligee as JAMISON enters. JAMISON enters excitedly.*)

JAMISON. The Queen!

SPALDING. Present arms!

(*SPALDING, with DuBarry's cape in his hands, turns it quickly inside out and throws it over his shoulders. On its reverse side it is the same color as the capes worn by the musketeers — Someone from the orchestra tosses him a hat similar to those worn by the others, instantly the four men fall into line; stand at attention. In appearance they are four musketeers. The QUEEN bursts in, sees DuBarry, who immediately runs off.*)

MRS. RITTENHOUSE. May I inquire what has been going on here? Where is the King? I asked you where is the King?

RAVELLI. Somebody trumped him.

MRS. RITTENHOUSE. I repeat! Where is the King?

SPALDING. He's out on Queens Boulevard.

MRS. RITTENHOUSE. Who may I ask are you?

(*Intro into NUMBER: FOUR OF THREE MUSKETEERS.*)

WE'RE FOUR OF THE THREE MUSKETEERS
WE'VE BEEN TOGETHER FOR YEARS
EENIE, MEENIE, MINEE, (HONK)
FOUR OF THE THREE MUSKETEERS
WE LIVE BY THE SWORD, BY THE SEA, BY THE WAY,
AND WE FIGHT DAY AND NIGHT
AND WE SLEEP NIGHT AND DAY.
MY COUNTRY TIS OF THEE
LAND OF THE LIGHT WINES AND BEERS
WE'RE CHEERED FROM DES MOINES TO ALGIERS
EACH TIME OUR MOTTO APPEARS
IT'S ONE FOR ALL AND TWO FOR FIVE
WE'RE FOUR OF THE THREE MUSKETEERS.

WHEN THE QUEEN NEEDS RECREATION
AND SHE STROLLS ALONG THE PATH
WHERE ARE WE?
RIGHT BY HER SIDE!
WHEN SHE'S FILLED WITH JUBILATION
OR CONSUMED WITH RAGTIME WRATH
WHERE ARE WE
RIGHT BY HER SIDE
WE'VE SWORN THAT WE'D SHIELD AND PROTECT HER
WE'RE HER GUARDSMEN, TRUE AND TRIED,
WHEN SHE GETS UP IN THE MORNING
AND SHE SLIPS INTO HER BATH
WHERE ARE WE?
FAR FROM THE OLD FOLKS AT HOME.

WE'RE FOUR OF THE THREE MUSKETEERS
WE'VE BEEN TOGETHER FOR YEARS.
IT'S ONE FOR ALL AND TWO FOR FIVE.
WE'RE FOUR OF THE THREE MUSKETEERS.

(*As number ends, enter HIVES in "Wig".*)

HIVES. (*with hidden glee*) Monsieur at Madame Beaugard have arrived.

(*JOHN enters carrying statue, MARY with him. They push past HIVES, MARY grabs HIVES' wig, puts it on JOHN who kneels before MRS. RITTENHOUSE. Two POLICE-MEN and DOUCET enter, push past HIVES.*)

DOUCET. Arrest the man! I demand that you . . . (*POLICE-MEN move to JOHN.*)
MARY. (*to POLICE*) Wait!
JOHN. (*handing statue to MRS. RITTENHOUSE, with an edge of vindication*) Your majesty, as a humble representative of the artists of France, each of whom is privileged to call you patron and friend, I beg that you will accept this, my latest effort.
MRS. RITTENHOUSE. Why this—this is the BEAUGARD. Monsieur Doucet—the BEAUGARD! (*Excitement and exclamations—*"What?" "The Beaugard, It's the Beaugard".)
(*simultaneously*)
DOUCET. Arrest them!   MARY. No! You mustn't!

(*General commotion. Enter SPALDING with statue, RA-VELLI and JAMISON with third statue.*)

CHANDLER. Is this a trick?
SPALDING. It certainly is. And a darn good one, too. We will now continue with sawing a woman in half.
RAVELLI. Mrs. Rittenhouse.
MRS. RITTENHOUSE. But what does all this mean?
MARY. (*pulling free of POLICEMEN*) I'll tell you (*pointing to the statue SPALDING carries*) This is the Beaugard . . . (*pointing to the statue JOHN brought in*) This one was done by John. (*DOUCET and CHANDLER examine both.*)
DOUCET. What? MonDieu,   CHANDLER. Why young C'est incroyable!   man you are a great sculptor.
DOUCET. (*to JOHN*) Then where did you get the Beaugard?
JOHN. From the Professor.
DOUCET. (*vengefully, to PROFESSOR*) Then you stole it?

Arrest him! (*Bit with POLICE and PROFESSOR. They grab his coat and he runs out of it.*)

JOHN. No! He found it in the room of—(*Turns to PROFESSOR, PROFESSOR grabs wig from JOHN, points to wig and then to HIVES. All exclaim "HIVES." HIVES bows as POLICE go to him.*)

SPALDING. Well everything is clearing up nicely. In ten minutes I'll be in a speakeasy.

DOUCET. But then who did the imitation—the bad one? (*PROFESSOR runs to GRACE, whistling and pointing. MARY points to GRACE who stands applying lip-stick with her left hand.*)

MARY. Look!

ALL. The left-handed sculptor.

GRACE. I knew it all the time. (*JAMISON enters.*)

JAMISON. Telegram! Telegram for Mr. Kabibble.

CHANDLER. Here you are boy. (*takes telegram*) Mazel tov! It is from the President. I am appointed the new minister to Czecho-Slovakia. He read about me in the "Traffic".

ARABELLA. All the big men read the Traffic.

CHANDLER. Young man, you are hired again at a big salary—

ARABELLA. And it's all my fault.

WINSTON. You bet it is.

CHANDLER. (*to JOHN*) And as for you my boy—your next commission is to chisel my bust.

MARY. It worked.

JOHN. You're wonderful.

SPALDING. And now friends I want to say—

FINALE: ACT 2
Reprise of HOORAY FOR CAPTAIN SPALDING

HOORAY FOR CAPTAIN SPALDING
HE FOUND THE PRICELESS BEAUGARD.
  SPALDING.
DID SOME ONE CALL ME: BLOW HARD?
  OMNES.
HOORAY, HOORAY, HOORAY
FROM CLIMATES HOT AND SCALDING
HE CAME AND SAVED OUR PARTY
WE RAISE OUR VOICES HEARTY
TO SING HOORAY, HOORAY.

Mrs. Rittenhouse.
HE'S ENDED OUR ANXIETY
AND SAVED OUR HIGH SOCIETY
FROM SHAMELESS IMPROPRIETY
Spalding.
HEY, HEY.
Omnes.
WITH FORTITUDE UNBENDING
HE'S BROUGHT A HAPPY ENDING
HE'S SHOWN AGAIN THAT HE'S OUR MAN
AND THAT IS WHY WE SAY.
HOORAY, HOORAY, HOORAY.
HOORAY!

CURTAIN

PROP LIST

ACT ONE, Scene 1
(10) Trays (Butlers) — w/handles
Doucet's luggage (Ishee) — 1 pc — small, black
Doucet's statue crate (Thole, Ishee)
Grace's luggage (Caleb) — 1 pc — round, overnite
Whitehead's luggage (Monroe) — 1 pc
(3) Newspapers (Guests) — tabloid, 1929, Morning Traffic
(2) Luggage (John Parker) — beat-up suitcase; artist bag
Wrapped statue (John Parker)
Salver (Hives) — silver
(2) Chandler's luggage (Caleb) — (2) suitcases
Chandler's golf clubs (Monroe)
Notepad & pencil (Winston)
(2) Scimitars (Scouts) — 1 long, 1 short
Carpet bag (Professor) — w/built-in clanks
Baseball bat & glove (Hives)
Pocket watch w/fob (Spalding)
(10) watches (Professor) — on velcro strip
Fez/beard (Professor) — attached w/elastic
Gun (Professor) — western toy pistol
Birthmark (Chandler) — red contact paper
Paper money (Chandler) — $500
Rubber check (Chandler) — $5000 check part
Rubber check (Professor) — magic part w/mortite
Teeth (Professor) — Chatter
Birthmark (Professor) — red contact paper
(2) Horns (Professor) — 1 — short, curved; 1 — long, straight
Riding crop (Jamison)
Tennis racket (Chandler)
Party blower (Professor)
Trombone (Ravelli)
Home plate (Hives)
Camera bag w/flash unit attached (Mary)
Mary's suitcase (Hives)
Notebook w/pencil attached (Hives)
(2) Clothes brushes (Caleb, Monroe) — small wisk type
Contract (Spalding)
Glasses (Mary) — Prescription
Glasses (Spalding) — no glass
Butterfly net (Professor)
Salt container (Professor)
Bell (Hives) — small

SCENE 3

Blackjack (Professor)

Deck of cards w/6 aces of spades (Professor) — 28 in deck; 1 torn each performance; marked on back

Trick card table (Hives) — velcro top

(2) Grace's statues w/pink teddy on 1 sheet

Stepladder (John Caleb/Professor)

Fish (Professor)

Flask (Professor) — silver

Flute (Professor)

(5) Playing cards (Professor) — flush oversize

Flashlight (Professor) — long, working

John's statue w/sheet

(3) "Cheers" chairs (Professor) — Act II breakfast chairs

Rope (Professor) — hemp in coil

Flitz (or spray pump) (Professor)

Tag — on chest; "Grand Rapids"

Umbrella (Hives)

Magnifying glass (Professor) — oversize

Camera (Mary) — w/working flash

(2) Flashbulbs (Mary)

Deck of cards (Ravelli)

Broom (Professor) — small

Dustpan (Professor)

Tablecloth (Hives) — stapled to pallet

Veil apparatus w/veil

ACT TWO, SCENE 1

(8) Breakfast place settings — attached to tables

(4) Vases — attached to tables

(4) Bouquets of flowers (Hives) — small, for vases

(2) Newspapers (Winston/Chandler) — "Morning Traffic"

Tray (Hives) — gold

Telegram #1 w/envelope (Hives) — "good news" text p. 74

(2) Paper money (Winston)

Telegram #2 w/envelope (Hives) — "bad news" text p. 78

Notebook & pencil (Jamison)

Chloroform bottle (Hives)

Chloroform rag (Hives)

(20) Cloud hands; (10) cloud heads

Policeman's whistle (Donovan)

Telescope (Spalding)

(3) Dinner napkins (Spalding, Ravelli, Jamison)
(2) Small white flags (Spalding, Ravelli)
Wine glass (Whitehead) — w/water
Pitch pipe — lives at V3

SCENE 3
Wine table w/1 Champagne bottle, 2 Champagne glasses
  (Jamison)
Sandwich (Ravelli) — fake, hoagie
Telegram #3 (no envelope) (Jamison) — for Chandler
1 Pillow — on poof
Compact w/mirror (Grace)
French theatre staff (Hives)
Scroll (Jamison) — dinner check text p. 123

FINAL FURNITURE LIST

ACT ONE, Scene 1
(1) Chandelier
Sedan Chair
Bird cage

Scene 2
Table — 3'6" diameter
(4) chairs — 1 w/reinforced back
(2) "Lotus" Lamps
Piano — Kiwai on platform
Settee

Scene 3
Magic chest

ACT TWO, Scene 1
(4) Breakfast tables — w/table cloths
(8) chairs — brass "bentwoods"
(4) Chandeliers — North, South, East, West

Scene 2
Harp
Dream panels

Scene 3
Poof — w/secret drawer
Wine table

SMALLER PROPS

ACT ONE, Scene 1
Butler/Maid—feather dusters, dust cloths, trays
Newspapers for girls
Luggage for guests
Doucet—statue crate
John—statue pkg
John—bags
Chandler—bags
G & W—bags
Winston—personals
Spalding's entrance—scout's gun(s)
G & W—statue pkg

Scene 2
Nothing special

Scene 3
Trick card TT
Cards/crayon
Harpo props—list as in text
Stealing sequence, 1-3-58—step ladder, tools, umbrella, fish,
    flask, flute, flush, flash light
3 "cheers" chairs for Harpo
Veiled sculpture
3 sculptures

ACT TWO, Scene 1
Breakfast—4 tables set for breakfast w/No food; 8 place
    settings; flowers on each table
Newspaper—Chandler
Tray w/orange juice—Hives
2 telegrams
Riding crop—Spalding
Pen & paper—Jamison
Chloroform bottle, handkerchief
Pix of horse
3 sculptures
Alarm clock w/strap—Harpo
16 cloud puppets (8 pr.)
Spray pump for Harpo

SCENE 2
Human harp

SCENE 3
Pageant — King's bed — pillows etc.
Racing form
Champagne bottle, tray, 2 glasses
Musketeers swords
3 statues
Ravelli sandwich
Royal dispatch
Handcuffs

SET PROPS

ACT ONE, SCENE 1
2 chandeliers V 1 & 3
Spalding's letter
The magic chest
Bird cage for listening

SCENE 2
Table
4 chairs

SCENE 3
2 "lotus" lamps
Same table & 4 chairs as Iii
Piano — kiwai
Setee
Door plug

ACT TWO, SCENE 1
4 Café tables
8 chairs
4 chandeliers
Magic chest
Door plug

SCENE 2
Human harp
Billowing dream panels

Scene 3
Panels trip to form canope
King's "bed" w/pillows
Door plug out

PRELIMINARY COSTUME LIST

ACT ONE, SCENE 1
Pith helmet (Spalding)
Tear away cape & suit (Professor)
Tear away dress (Guest)
Handkerchief (Chandler)
Tie (Chandler) — easily removable
Tie (Ravelli) — easily removable
Tie (Professor) — easily removable

SCENE 3
Chemise (Mrs. Whitehouse) — easily removable

ACT TWO, SCENE 3
Reversible cape — DuBarry — Musketeer
Musketeer hat (Spalding)
Wig (Hives — Parker)

COSTUME PLOT

ACT ONE, SCENE 1

HIVES
Black tails
Black vest
White shirt
White tie
Black pants w/suspenders
Black shoes
Black socks

HAREM GIRL
Headband w/coins
Sequin bra
Orange pantie
Orange harem pants
Coin belt
Gold slippers

ENSEMBLE
BUTLER:
Black & charcoal striped pants w/suspenders
White shirt w/studs
Black bow tie
Grey vest
Black tail coat
Black socks
Black shoes
Undershirt
BIRD:
Yellow unitard
Feather & sequin headress
Feather waist schmata
Feather wristlets
Feather anklets

GUEST
Beige w/brn striped suit
Brown belt
Tan w/brown striped shirt
Brown shoes
Brown socks
Gray hat
Remove hat after opening

RAVELLI
    Plaid pants w/suspenders
    Striped shirt
    Red & black tie
    Brown corduroy jacket
    Traditional hat
    Black hi-tops
    Black socks

DOUCET
    Lt. blue tailored suit
    White shirt
    White socks
    White shoes
    Lt. blue tie
    Cream beret
    Pencil mustache

SCOUT, POLICEMAN
SCOUT:
    Pink tunic
    Pink over-tunic w/gold & black stripes
    Pink waist wrap
    Gold neck piece
    Pink & gold turban

HAREM GIRL; GUEST; STATUE
GUEST:
    Blue patterned dress
    Blue slip
    Tights
    Dance briefs
    Tan characters
    Blond wig
HAREM:
    Headband w/coins
    Sequin bra
    Blue panties
    Blue harem pants
    Coin belt
    Silver slippers
    Brown harem wig

ENSEMBLE
BUTLER:
  Blk & charcoal striped pants w/suspenders
  White shirt w/studs
  Black bow tie
  Grey vest
  Black tail coat
  Black socks
  Black shoes
  Undershirt
GUEST:
  Brn & white weave suit w/vest
  Suspenders
  Red, magenta & yellow tie
  Lt. tan shirt
BIRD:
  Yellow unitard
  Feather & sequin headress
  Feather waist schmata
  Feather wristlets
  Feather anklets
  Yellow ballet slippers

CHANDLER
  Blk cutaway coat
  White shirt
  Grey & white striped tie
  Black vest
  Charcoal & black pants
  Black shoes
  Black socks
  Handkerchief

MRS. RITTENHOUSE
  Blue lace evening dress
  Seamed hose
  Black shoes
  Long pearl necklace
  Pearl earrings
  Brunette wig
  Body padding

ENSEMBLE
BUTLER:
  Blk & charcoal striped pants w/suspenders
  White shirt w/studs
  Black bow tie
  Grey vest
  Black tail coat
  Black knee-hi socks
  Black shoes
  Strawberry blond wig
GUEST:
  Raw sienna print dress
  Rust & green hat
  Tan characters
  Slip
BIRD:
  Yellow unitard
  Feather & sequin headress
  Feather waist schmata
  Feather wristlets
  Feather anklets
  Yellow ballet slippers

GUEST; HAREM GIRL; STATUE
GUEST:
  Pink satin dress
  Hose
  Tan shoes
  Blond wig
  Slip
  Pink hat
HAREM:
  Headband w/coins
  Sequin bra
  Pink panties
  Pink harem pants
  Coin belt
  Gold slippers
  Blond harem wig

ENSEMBLE
BUTLER:
  Blk & charcoal striped pants w/suspenders

White shirt w/studs
Black bow tie
Grey vest
Black tail coat
Black socks
Black shoes
Undershirt

GUEST:
Brn suit w/vest
Lt pink shirt
Brn, orange & white tie
Brn characters

BIRD:
Yellow unitard
Feather & sequin headress
Feather waist schmata
Feather anklets
Feather wristlets
Yellow ballet slippers

CAPTAIN SPALDING
Pith helmet
Black tail coat
White shirt w/curled collar
Black tie
Short, tan riding pants
Black boots
Glasses
Black socks
Sock garters
Greasepaint mustache & eyebrows

ENSEMBLE
BUTLER:
Blk & charcoal striped pants w/suspenders
White shirt w/studs
Black bow tie
Grey vest
Black tail coat
Black socks
Black shoes
Undershirt

BIRD:
    Yellow unitard
    Feather & sequin headress
    Feather waist schmata
    Feather anklets
    Feather wristlets

ARABELLA
    Lt purple print dress
    Lavendar slip
    Long pearl necklace
    Dance tights
    Dance briefs
    Tan characters
    Blond wig
    Lt purple headband

PROFESSOR
    Blk top hat
    Blk breakaway cape & trousers
    Black socks
    Blk sock garters
    Black shoes
    White shirtfront
    Black bow tie
    "Harpo" wig
    Whale underwear
Traditional:
    Tan overcoat
    Grey check pants w/suspenders
    Striped shirt
    Black & yellow tie (hat design)
    Brown belt

GRACE CARPENTER
    Beige coat, fur collar
    Cream hat w/rose
    Cream gloves
    Cream purse
    Gold dress
    Seamed hose
    Black shoes
    Slip
    Black wig

ENSEMBLE
BUTLER:
  Blk & charcoal striped pants w/suspenders
  White shirt w/studs
  Black bow tie
  Grey vest
  Black tail coat
  Black socks
  Black shoes
  Dark brunette wig
GUEST:
  Rust breakaway dress
  Blue teddy
  Dance tights
  Tan characters
  Rust hat
BIRD:
  Yellow unitard
  Feather & sequin headress
  Feather waist schamata
  Feather anklets
  Feather wristlets
  Yellow ballet slippers

GUEST; HAREM GIRL; STATUE
GUEST:
  Blue-grey print dress
  Hose
  Brown shoes
  Blue-grey hat
  Brown wig
HAREM GIRL:
  Headband w/coins
  Sequin bra
  Green panties
  Green harem pants
  Coin belt
  Silver slippers
  Brown harem wig

ENSEMBLE
BUTLER:
  Blk & charcoal striped pants w/suspenders

White shirt w/studs
Black bow tie
Grey vest
Black tail coat
Black socks
Black shoes

GUEST:
Grey print dress
Grey hat
Dance tights
Slip
Tan characters

BIRD:
Yellow unitard
Feather & sequin headress
Feather waist schmata
Feather anklets
Feather wristlets
Yellow ballet slippers

ENSEMBLE
BUTLER:
Blk & charcoal striped pants w/suspenders
White shirt w/studs
Black bow tie
Grey vest
Black tail coat
Black socks
Black shoes
Brown wig

GUEST:
Tan print dress
Dance tights
Tan characters
Rust hat

BIRD:
Yellow unitard
Feather & sequin headress
Feather waist schmata
Feather anklets
Feather wristlets
Yellow ballet slippers

JAMISON
    Tan safari suit w/belt
    Brown safari hat
    Brown boots
    Putees
    Undershirt

MARY
    Cream crocheted tam
    Lt. blue jacket
    Lt. blue polka-dot dress
    Seamed hose
    Tan T-strap shoes
    Slip
    Red wig

ENSEMBLE
BUTLER:
    Blk & charcoal striped pants w/suspenders
    White shirt w/studs
    Grey vest
    Black bow tie
    Black tail coat
    Black socks
    Black shoes
    Dk. brown wig
GUEST:
    Green satin dress
    Tan hat
    Fox fur piece
    Tan characters
    Dance tights
BIRD:
    Yellow unitard
    Feather & sequin headress
    Feather waist schmata
    Feather anklets
    Feather wristlets
    Yellow ballet slippers

SCOUT; POLICEMAN
SCOUT:
    Turquoise pants
    Gold anklets

Turquoise print waist wrap
Gold turban
Gold & turquoise neckpiece
Black & gold over tunic

ENSEMBLE
BUTLER:
Blk & charcoal striped pants w/suspenders
White shirt w/studs
Grey vest
Black bow tie
Black tail coat
Black socks
Black shoes
Undershirt
GUEST:
Brn plaid suit
White sweater
Tan shirt
Wine suspenders
Yellow & blue
Tan tie characters
BIRD:
Yellow unitard
Feather & sequin headress
Feather waist schmata
Feather anklets
Feather wristlets
Yellow ballet slippers

WALLY WINSTON
Tan slacks
Blue shirt
Navy patterned tie
Check sports jacket
Brown shoes
Brown socks
Straw boater

MRS. WHITEHEAD
Grey coat w/fur collar
Lemon hat
Grey purse
Grey gloves

Grey & yellow dress w/petal skirt
Green alligator shoes
Slip
Black wig

JOHN PARKER
Grey slacks
Off white shirt
Suspenders
Navy & white tie
Black shoes
Black socks
Add:
Grey jacket

SCENE 2

HIVES
Same as I;1

HAREM GIRL
Same as I;1

CHANDLER
Same as I;1

CAPTAIN SPALDING
Traditional:
Black pants
White shirt
Black tie
Black tail coat
Black socks
Black shoes

SCENE 3

HIVES
Same as I;1

HAREM GIRL
Same as I;1

ENSEMBLE
GUEST:
Med. brown suit
Pink shirt

Pink, maroon, white tie
Tan tap shoes

GUEST
Same as I;1
Add:
Tan tap shoes

RAVELLI
Same as I;1

DOUCET
Same as I;1

SCOUT; POLICEMAN
Same as I;1

HAREM GIRL; GUEST; STATUE
GUEST:
Add:
Tan tap shoes

ENSEMBLE
GUEST:
w/tap shoes

CHANDLER
Same as I;1

MRS. RITTENHOUSE
Same as I;1

ENSEMBLE
GUEST:
w/tan tap shoes
Remove:
Hat

GUEST; HAREM GIRL; STATUE
GUEST:
Remove:
Hat

ENSEMBLE
GUEST:
w/tap shoes

CAPTAIN SPALDING
  Traditional

ENSEMBLE
GUEST:
  Med. tan & white suit
  Brn, pink & mauve tie
  Lt. tan shirt
  Tan tap shoes

ARABELLA
  Purple dress w/handkerchief hem
  Satin shoes
  Purple headband

PROFESSOR
  Traditional

GRACE CARPENTER
  Same as I;1
Remove:
  Hat, coat, gloves, purse

ENSEMBLE
GUEST:
  Dk. turquoise print dress
  Dance tights
  Dance briefs
  Tan tap shoes

GUEST; HAREM GIRL; STATUE
GUEST:
Remove:
  Hat

ENSEMBLE
GUEST:
  w/tap shoes:
Remove:
  Hat

ENSEMBLE
GUEST:
  w/tap shoes
Remove:
  Hat

JAMISON
Same as I;1

MARY
Same as I;1
Remove:
Tan jacket

ENSEMBLE
GUEST:
w/tap shoes
Remove:
Hat & fur

ENSEMBLE
GUEST:
w/tap shoes

WALLY WINSTON
Same as I;1
Add:
Tap shoes

MRS. WHITEHEAD
Same as I;1
Remove:
Hat, coat, purse, gloves
Add:
Removable chemise

JOHN PARKER
Same as I;1

ACT TWO, Scene 1

HIVES
Same as I;1

ENSEMBLE
CLOUD BUTLER:
Remove:
Jacket
Add:
Cumberbund
Bathing suit — forest green bottom, green plaid top; green belt

GUEST
  Same as I;1

RAVELLI
  Same as I;1
  Bathing suit — blue & green; striped (2) piece bathing suit

DOUCET
  Same as I;1

SCOUT; POLICEMAN
POLICEMAN:
  Navy blue uniform
  Lt. blue shirt
  Navy blue tie
  Navy blue hat
  Black belt
  Navy socks
  Black shoes

HAREM GIRL; GUEST; STATUE
STATUE:
  Nude bodystocking
  Nude hose
  Grey chiffon drape

ENSEMBLE
CLOUD BUTLER:
  Bathing suit — red & white striped top
  Navy bottoms
  Navy belt

CHANDLER
  Grey suit w/vest
  White shirt
  Print tie
  Suspenders
  Bathing suit — navy w/white trim — 1 piece

MRS. RITTENHOUSE
  Peach lace evening dress w/underdress
  Diamond bracelet
  Beach outfit — jumpsuit: grn. top, grn. & red print bottom;
    matching jacket; matching hat

ENSEMBLE
CLOUD BUTLER:
Bathing suit — sea green bottom, grn. & orange striped top,
white belt

GUEST w/teddy
STATUE:
Nude body stocking
Nude hose
Grey chiffon drape

CLOUD BUTLER:
Bathing suit — cream top, brn bottoms, white belt

CAPTAIN SPALDING
Riding outfit — jodphurs, short boots
Traditional coat, tie, shirt
Add:
Aviators cap & scarf
Bathing suit — black & white striped 1 piece
Black socks & garters
Black shoes

ENSEMBLE
CLOUD BUTLER:
Bathing suit — Brn & white striped top
Brn. bottom
White belt

ARABELLA
Same as I;3
Bathing suit — tangerine bottom; tangerine & white top
Tangerine headband
Tan characters

PROFESSOR
Traditional
Bathing suit — (upside down) lime green w/blue trim
Green belt
Add:
Traditional coat & pants

GRACE CARPENTER
Green dress w/flower print
Hose

Black shoes
Pearl necklace

ENSEMBLE
CLOUD BUTLER:
Bathing suit—pink bottom, pink & white striped top
White belt
Tan characters

GUEST; HAREM GIRL; STATUE
STATUE:
Nude body stocking
Nude hose
Grey chiffon drape

ENSEMBLE
CLOUD BUTLER:
Bathing suit—orange w/white trim 1 piece
Tan characters
White belt

ENSEMBLE
CLOUD BUTLER:
Bathing suit—yellow bottom, yellow & white & blue striped top
White belt
Tan characters

JAMISON
Dk. blue suit
Lt. blue shirt
Blue print tie
Black shoes
Black socks
Bathing suit—red & white striped 2 piece

MARY
Pink polka-dot dress w/solid pink skirt
Pink polka-dot jacket
Gold heart locket
Hose
Shoes
Slip

ENSEMBLE
CLOUD BUTLER:
Bathing suit—royal blue bottom; blue & red striped top

White belt
Tan characters

SCOUT; POLICEMAN
POLICEMAN:
Navy blue uniform
Lt. blue shirt
Navy blue tie
Navy blue hat
Black belt
Navy socks
Black shoes

ENSEMBLE
CLOUD BUTLER:
Bathing suit—blue bottom; blue, pink & white striped top
Maroon belt

WALLY WINSTON
Red jacket
Red patterned tie
Slacks
Shirt
Shoes
Socks
Boater

MRS. WHITEHEAD
White dress w/flower pattern
Hose
Slip
Shoes

JOHN PARKER
Same as I;1

ACT TWO, Scene 2

PROFESSOR
Traditional coat & pants w/bathing suit top

ENSEMBLE
HARP BALLET:
Gold lame leotard
Gold ballet slippers
Gold glitter
Wig

ACT TWO, Scene 3

HIVES
Add:
  White wig
  Black knickers
  Jabot
  Black tights

HAREM GIRL
  Same as I;1

GUEST
  Same as I;1

RAVELLI
MUSKETEER:
  Green hat w/plume
  Lt. green pants
  Lt. green vest
  Dk. green coat
  White jabot
  White wig
  Boots
Curtain Call:
  Remove musketeer hat & wig
  Add traditional hat

DOUCET
  Same as I;1

SCOUT; POLICEMAN
  Same as II;1

CHANDLER
  Suit f/II

MRS. RITTENHOUSE
QUEEN:
  Lavendar ball gown
  Hip roll
  White wig

CAPTAIN SPALDING
MUSKETEER:
  Rust hat w/white feathers
  Rust coat

Brn. sash
Brn. knickers
White jabot
White wig
Shoes, socks & garters f/II;1

PROFESSOR
MUSKETEER:
Orange hat
Orange knickers
White stockings
Gold vest
Orange jacket
White jabot
Remove:
Hat & coat
Add:
Traditional coat

GRACE CARPENTER
Same as II

JAMISON
MUSKETEER:
Blue knickers
Blue vest
Blue & gold cape
White jabot
White wig
Gold hat
Blue coat
Boots
Remove:
Hat & wig

MARY
Same as II

WALLY WINSTON
Same as II

MRS. WHITEHEAD
DUBARRY:
Orange ball gown
Hip roll